THE RECLUSE OF HERALD SQUARE

Mrs. Ida Wood in the 1860's

THE RECLUSE OF HERALD SQUARE

THE MYSTERY OF IDA E. WOOD

Joseph A. Cox

THE MACMILLAN COMPANY, NEW YORK

Third Printing, 1964

THE MACMILLAN COMPANY, NEW YORK

COLLIER-MACMILLAN CANADA LTD., TORONTO, ONTARIO

Library of Congress catalog card number: 64-17375

Printed in the United States of America

DESIGNED BY ANDREW P. ZUTIS

To my wife Jean

PREFACE

The Recluse of Herald Square, which narrates the search for Ida Wood, is a true story. The incredible deception which this remarkable woman practiced is further proof that truth can indeed be stranger than fiction. Despite the prominence which she achieved and the fortune she amassed, her secret remained unexposed during her lifetime. The drama of her death as a recluse, the discovery of her concealed fortune, and the search for her true identity made headline news in the 1930's. Ida Wood's story is a fascinating mystery.

It fell to me as counsel for the Public Administrator of New York County to supervise the long search in this country and abroad for Ida Wood's true identity, to ward off the more than one thousand false claimants to her fortune, and to distribute it to her real next of kin.

I acknowledge with thanks the assistance which I have received in writing the manuscript. Joseph T. Arenson, Thomas J. Nevins and Eve M. Preminger made many helpful suggestions. John Tebbel rendered valuable literary help. Mrs. Mary McGrath served as a faithful amanuensis. Completion of the manuscript was assisted by additional research in which I engaged under the auspices of Columbia University's Oral History Research Office, at whose request I recorded my experiences. I am grateful to my friend Ludwig Teller for his steadfast work and creative advice in the planning and the writing of the manuscript.

Joseph A. Cox

New York City
September, 1964

THE RECLUSE OF HERALD SQUARE

1

SHORTLY AFTER NOON on a bleak March day in 1932, a feeble but indomitable old lady closed her nearly blind eyes which had once looked upon Abraham Lincoln and the Prince of Wales, struggled briefly to retain a life she had always been able to shape to her own desires, and failing, slipped away to a death that was merciful if not welcome.

Thus began one of the strangest cases ever to come before the Surrogate's Court of New York County, a litigation unique in the annals of inheritance, and certainly one of the most incredible stories in the history of American jurisprudence.

The lady's name was Ida E. Wood. Even as she lay dying on an old iron bed in the Herald Square Hotel, she was a celebrated case in the Supreme Court of New York, where the struggle for her wealth had begun. For a year the newspapers had been full of her story, because the woman they called "The Recluse of Herald Square" was not merely an eccentric old lady who had retired to her hotel room shortly after the Panic of 1907 and never come out again, but a person of consequence in nineteenth century New York society. She had been the owner of a leading newspaper; she had moved in the inner circles of city politics. Most of all, she was leaving a large fortune—no one yet knew exactly how much.

In her last days, Ida's exhausted, disconnected mind had been dwelling in the past, dredging up fragments of recollection from the ninety-four years of her astonishing existence. She liked to talk about her dead husband, Benjamin Wood, the proprietor of the New York *Daily News* (unrelated to its modern namesake), a paper so rabid in its Southern sympathies during the Civil War that Ben was nearly indicted for treason. Nevertheless, Ida was proud that her husband had served in the New York State Senate and the United States House of Representatives, although in Washington his pro-Southern conduct had involved him in sharp controversy with his colleagues.

Ida talked about Ben, and occasionally about her husband's brother, Fernando Wood, a noted and notorious mayor of New York City who had shared Ben's political beliefs and helped to make his brother rich. She spoke also of meeting Lincoln and entertaining President Cleveland and dancing with the Prince of Wales and socializing with the Empress Eugenie. She mentioned other family matters, often mysteriously and confusedly. Clearly there was much more to Ida than met the eye, sympathetic or calculating, that surveyed her wasted, pathetic body as it lay near death.

Remembering her rich and glittering life, it was a melancholy thing to see her now in the dark, cluttered hotel room. The woman who had once been a reigning beauty, whose face and figure had ornamented the most exclusive ballrooms, was withered away. She weighed no more than seventy pounds, and her tiny body was lost in her pale blue flannelette nightgown. Long white hair partly covered her face.

In a semicoma, she lay on her right side, knees drawn up nearly to her chin in the embryonic position the dying so often assume, returning as they leave to the prenatal posture. A cheap woolen blanket and a white counterpane covered Ida E. Wood, and she slept beneath them in total retreat at last from a world she no longer cared about.

Outside a raw March wind harried the shoppers who struggled through the snow and ice still on the pavement in that frigid winter. When Ida was in her prime, Herald Square at Thirty-fourth Street, formed by the intersection of Broadway and the Avenue of the Americas (then Sixth Avenue), had been the crossroads of New York and the heart of the theater district, but now its earlier glories were as far in the past as Ida's. The Herald Square Hotel, which was somewhat west of Herald Square, had been built in 1898, about the time she had become the owner of her husband's newspaper. Like Ida, it had known its splendors, when the great names of the theater had occupied some of its 273 spacious rooms, and those who applauded them had dined in its sumptuous restaurant before and after the play. Now the hotel and Ida were dying together. Dwarfed by Macy's and Gimbel's and squeezed in by other business establishments, it was a brick-and-brownstone anachronism, already marked for the wrecking crew.

In common with everyone else who read the papers, I was fascinated by the strange story of the Recluse of Herald Square. In those days I was Counsel to the New York County Public Administrator, James F. Egan, and as a lawyer engaged in estate matters I had a special interest in reading about the anticipated battle over the substantial sum Ida was expected to leave when she died. I had no idea I would be one of the actors in the drama that would unfold after her death, and would spend much of my time for the next several years in a search for Ida's identity.

It was to be, as I soon discovered, an unprecedented search. Before her rightful heirs would be finally determined in 1939, a total of 1,103 persons from every part of the United States and several foreign countries would come forward to contend that they were her nearest relatives. Scores of attorneys would produce a mountain of evidence to support these claims, and the court record would run to thousands of pages.

The search for heirs had really begun before Ida drew her last breath. Attorneys searching her possessions had found a will dated July 9, 1889, a cracked and yellow document under which her entire estate would be shared equally by her daughter Emma Wood and her sister Mary Mayfield.

Unfortunately for Ida's original intention, both these legatees died before she did. As one who had followed the unfolding story in the papers with some fascination, I knew what was generally known about these two ladies, but the little that was known only sharpened my interest, for Mary and Emma by this time were figures almost as mysterious as Ida herself.

It had been Mary's death, a year before, which had suddenly projected Ida into the world again after twenty-four years of nearly complete seclusion in the Herald Square Hotel. Only necessity had moved her to renew contact with that world she had resolutely shut out for so long. On March 5, 1931, she had unbolted and opened the door, peered down the dingy hall, and called the chambermaid.

Margaret Kilkenny, the floor maid, could not have been more surprised to hear herself summoned. Ida had never opened her door voluntarily except to take food brought up by the night elevator operator; a succession of floor maids had never been able to get into the room to clean it. Dirty sheets and towels were passed through a narrowly opened door in exchange for clean ones.

But now, at four o'clock in the afternoon, Ida's voice shrilled down the corridor: "Maid, come here. My sister is sick."

Surprised, and a little reluctant, Margaret Kilkenny shuffled down the threadbare carpet of the corridor to suite 551–552, where Ida lived. The door was open no more than two inches; Ida obviously had no intention of letting her in.

"My sister is sick," Ida repeated harshly. "Get a doctor. I think she's going to die." Then she slammed the door in her customary fashion, and the maid could hear the two bolts being shot into place.

Miss Kilkenny went down to the lobby and approached the hotel's manager, Stanley Rogers.

"One of them in 552 is sick," she told him. "They asked me to get a doctor."

Since the Herald Square had no resident doctor of its own, Mr. Rogers called the Hotel McAlpin nearby, at Sixth Avenue and Thirty-fourth Street, to get the house physician there. An hour later he appeared. To Dr. Howell E. Babcock, blond and bespectacled, it was a routine call; he had been taking care of the hotel's patients as well as the McAlpin's for several years.

When he came to 552, Dr. Babcock found the door open slightly, and as he raised his hand to knock, it swung open far enough to reveal a small, wraithlike woman whose white hair was long and matted. It was Ida.

"Who are you?" she inquired suspiciously, in a sharp, high-pitched voice.

The doctor identified himself, peering a little uneasily at the apparition confronting him. Ida seemed reassured.

"It's my sister Mary," she said. "I think she's going to die."

Dr. Babcock moved to enter the room, but Ida blocked him by pushing the door nearly shut in his face.

"How much are you going to charge?" she demanded.

"If you can't pay," the doctor answered diplomatically, "I certainly won't charge you anything."

"Oh, I'll pay you," Ida said, "but I warn you, not more than three dollars."

With that she opened the door enough for the doctor to squeeze in. He found himself in a darkened room, illuminated only by the light from the hall. Feeling along the wall by the door he found the switch and turned on the room's overhead fixture.

With a sense of shock, he could see Ida clearly for the first time, her face remarkably smooth but with skin tightly drawn, her pointed nose and chin, and her eyes, bright, penetrating, alive, and suspicious.

The room itself was like nothing Dr. Babcock had ever seen. He was standing in the only cleared space. The remainder was piled high with dust-laden rubbish. Piles of magazines and papers, packages and cardboard boxes of every shape and size, hatboxes and valises, barrels, trunks, a few wooden boxes, rolls of carpeting, bundles of what looked like yellow portieres—all were thrown together in indescribable confusion.

There were a few chairs in the room, but they were buried under heaping stacks of old books, magazines, and packages of correspondence tied with ribbon and string. An ancient, dilapidated rocker was the only place remaining to sit. In one corner, barricaded by piles of bundles, was what passed for a sofa, but it was no more than a shapeless heap of old sheets, blankets, afghans, and comforters. Some of them obviously had not been washed or cleaned for years. A shelf ran along one wall. It was piled with litter reaching nearly to the ceiling. A small space had been cleared at one end to hold a china cup, two small china plates, a few pieces of tarnished black silver, a drinking glass, and a small saucepan. Below, on a dusty trunk, was a two-burner, grime-covered electric stove.

Surveying this dismal scene with incredulous eyes, Dr. Babcock recovered his professional poise long enough to ask, "Where's your sister?"

Ida moved to a door at the right of the room, which she unlocked with a key and swung open. "She's in there," Ida said.

The second room was nearly as littered as the first, and it was illuminated by an even smaller bulb. Dimly, Dr. Babcock could see an emaciated old woman lying on a cot. She was wearing a ragged nightgown, and the doctor's practiced eye noted that she was in a comatose condition. Bending over her, he saw that she was scarcely breathing. He guessed that she weighed no more than seventy-five pounds. There was not much doubt about her condition. Prodding gently around the great swelling in her abdomen, it was plain to the doctor that his patient was dying of a cancer that was in its terminal stage.

"I'm afraid there's nothing I can do here," he said. "Your sister should be in a hospital."

"No, no," Ida protested sharply. "I don't want her moved out of here. You can go now."

They moved back into Ida's room, and Dr. Babcock took out his pad and fountain pen.

"May I have your name, please?" he asked politely.

Ida regarded him suspiciously. "What do you want it for?"

"I have to make a record of this call," the doctor explained patiently. "And I have to have your sister's name."

"I'm Ida Wood." She was suddenly talkative. "My husband was Benjamin Wood. His brother was mayor of New York."

Dr. Babcock wrote down her name and made no comment. Senility, he thought.

"And what is your sister's name?"

"Her name is Mary Mayfield. She never married, and she's ninety-one years old. I'm ninety-three."

"How long have you lived in this hotel?"

"Twenty-four years," Ida said. "I never go out, you know. And I never let anyone in. Mary used to go out some, but she won't any more."

While she volunteered this information, Ida had slumped into her chair, and was rocking slowly back and forth. As he picked up his hat and bag, a professional impulse moved Dr. Babcock to take one more look at Mary Mayfield. He came out in a moment and said to Ida, "I'm sorry, Mrs. Wood, but your sister is dead."

Ida stopped rocking. "Oh, dear," she said petulantly. "Now she'll have to be buried, and that will cost money."

There was no room in Ida's disordered mind for normal grief, although she and Mary had been devoted to each other all their lives. In the dim region of extreme age in which she now lived, Ida's thoughts and emotions were stripped to elementals.

When Mr. Rogers appeared at the suite in response to the doctor's call, she told him bluntly at once: "I want an undertaker. Not a fancy one. Just somebody who will bury Mary."

The manager stared at her, dumbfounded. He had been in his job a little more than six years, during which he had never seen either Ida or her sister Mary. He knew of their existence, of course; they were the curiosity of the hotel. The establishment's records had told him that they had checked into the Herald Square in 1907, accompanied by Mrs. Wood's daughter Emma. The records showed, too, that they had always paid their bills in cash, although usually it took repeated calls and dunning messages to get the money.

Mr. Rogers recalled Emma's death in 1928, but there had been no disturbance about it at the hotel, because she had been removed to a hospital and died there, at the age of seventy-one. Seeing Emma when they carried her out to the ambulance was the only time Mr. Rogers had ever set eyes on any of his three tenants in 552. He had worried about the situation from time to time, but there was little he could do about it. William Henry Grant, the night elevator operator, brought them food every few days; he was the only one in the hotel who had ever been inside the suite. Ida would call him, give him a little money, and send him to a delicatessen for bacon, eggs, coffee, crackers, butter, evaporated milk, and fish. She always ordered the same list.

Every time he went on this errand, Grant had told his boss, Ida never failed to tell him that the money she gave him was the last she had in the world, and she didn't know what she was going to do now that her cash was gone.

When he returned with the groceries, she always tipped him a dime.

Knowing this much about his tenants, Mr. Rogers was not surprised to hear that Ida wasn't in the market for a fancy undertaker. But he did what was usually done when someone in the hotel died, and an undertaker was required. He called P. B. McDonnell, whose funeral home was nearby. When Mr. McDonnell came, the two men went back to the suite, and succeeded in getting in after pounding awhile on the door.

There followed a frustrating hour or so during which Ida simply refused to talk to them. She sat bent over in her rocker, head bowed, oblivious to their explanations, pleas, and exhortations. At last she stared up at them through her white hair and said, "Call Judge O'Brien. He always handled matters for my husband. I don't see why he can't handle this for me."

It took more prodding and prying from the two men to extract from Ida the necessary further information that the judge's first name was Morgan, and that he lived in Manhattan. By this time it was past midnight, but Mr. McDonnell decided it would be best to make the call. He found a Morgan J. O'Brien, Jr., listed in the directory at 729 Park Avenue.

It was this Mr. O'Brien who answered the phone. Judge O'Brien, he explained, was his father, retired from practice and at the moment vacationing in Florida. The younger O'Brien had never heard of Ida or her sisters, but he promised to get in touch with his father next day and see if something could be done. Somewhat reassured, McDonnell did what he could in the suite. He covered Mary's body with a sheet and moved it, cot and all, into the parlor, leaving the bedroom for Ida.

Next day young Mr. O'Brien, a member of the distinguished law firm of O'Brien, Boardman, Conboy, Memhard and Early, succeeded in reaching his father. The judge was astonished to hear that Ida was still alive. "I remember her well," he told his son. "She was a beauty, I can tell you, the belle of society in my time. She was one of the best known women in New York. And a smart businesswoman too. Your mother and I occasionally entertained her and her sister."

During the 1880's, before he became a Supreme Court Justice, the judge went on, he had handled legal matters for both Ben and Ida, but he understood that Ida had taken all her money out of the banks, and converted her assets into cash shortly before the Panic of 1907. He had never heard a word from her after that, and had assumed she was dead. "Do what you can for her, Morgan," he said. "I always liked her."

What Morgan O'Brien, Jr. did immediately was to call McDonnell and instruct him to go ahead with the funeral. Then he called one of the firm's lawyers, Harold G. Wentworth, a specialist in the handling of estates, and told him to meet him at the Herald Square Hotel. With that call, the door swung open at last on the strange private world of the Recluse of Herald Square, and the life of Ida E. Wood began to rise to the surface, like some lost Atlantis emerging from the submerged depths of the past.

2

WHEN THE TWO lawyers knocked on the door of 552, it was opened at once, a most unusual occurrence in itself. That was because McDonnell the undertaker was now its guardian, not Ida.

"She's in there," McDonnell said, indicating the bedroom. "She's locked herself in, and she won't come out," he added somewhat plaintively.

The lawyers glanced at each other. "We'll have to see if we can't persuade her," O'Brien said.

What followed was described later in court by Wentworth. "Perhaps after five or ten minutes of hammering," he testified, "the door opened, and the figure of an aged woman appeared. Her hair was very much disheveled, and she had a pronounced stoop. She was perhaps five feet tall, with the stoop, and she was very feeble. She had an old hotel towel pinned around the upper part of her body, and the lower portion was covered with material that enclosed it and was held together with pins or something. It was not a dress, as we know it. She had considerable difficulty in walking. She walked very, very slowly, and she came over to a chair and invited Mr. O'Brien, Jr., and myself to sit down. . . ."

Recalling that first meeting at another time, O'Brien said:

"When Mrs. Wood came out, I told her my name. She sat down in a rocking chair, and started massaging her face with this petroleum jelly we had heard about." (He had heard about it in a conversation with Rogers and other members of the hotel staff before the two men had come up to the room.) "I realized she was rather deaf. I kept shouting my name at her, and finally she seemed to understand what I was saying, and she got up and came over to me.

"She was very little, and was bent over like a question mark, but you could see she had once been a pretty woman, and her skin was smooth and unwrinkled. She couldn't see very well, apparently. She came up to me and felt my face all over with her hands, and then she drew back and exclaimed, 'You're not Judge O'Brien at all!' I tried to tell her I was Judge O'Brien's son, and she finally seemed to understand that.

"She sat down again, and lighted a long, thin cigar. She talked fairly sensibly and amiably for a while, although in a rather wandering fashion. She showed us some Union Pacific bonds and some uncashed dividend checks. She said her daughter and her sister had both had money in their own right, and had willed it to her. She hinted that she had a good deal of cash in the bedroom. I asked her if she had a bank account, and she said that she didn't have one now, but that she used to have one at the Morton Trust Company. She told me she had no relatives and no friends.

"But then, all at once, she sort of switched, and became very irate and hysterical. She called me an impostor and a crook, said I was just after her money, like everybody else, said she didn't like my voice or my looks, and didn't want a lawyer anyway. She told me to get out. Then she snatched up the shoebox full of bonds and papers, and hobbled with startling speed into the bedroom, and closed and locked the door. Wentworth and I hung around for a while, banging on the door and trying to get her to come out, but she wouldn't, so we finally went back to the office. Frankly, we didn't know what to do."

One of the things the O'Brien firm could do was to look into the sources of the wealth Ida had hinted at. Inquiry at the Union Pacific yielded the information that the sisters had owned about $175,000 worth of stock, and had not cashed their dividend checks for a dozen years. Examining the sale of Ben Wood's newspaper, which Ida had sold in 1901 to Frank Munsey, the publisher of the New York *Sun,* it was learned that the price was set tentatively at somewhere near $250,000; actually, it proved to be more.

An officer of the Guaranty Trust Company, who had known Ida when she banked at the Morton Trust, remembered the day in 1907 when she had appeared at the bank and closed her account, putting nearly a million dollars into a netted bag and marching out, never to be seen inside the bank's doors again.

It had not been an easy transaction. The Guaranty's officer, then a young teller at Morton Trust, remembered that Ida had come to his window demanding the balance of her account in cash. Since the amount was substantial, he had asked her to wait while he consulted an officer of the bank, who in turn consulted other officers. They decided that Ida could not have her entire balance. An officer assured her that her funds were safe in the bank, and remarked that it would be extremely dangerous for her to carry so large a quantity of cash.

"Is that your final decision?" Ida demanded coldly. They told her it was.

"If that's so," Ida told them, "then I will tell you what I'm going to do. I'll go to every newspaper in town and advise them that the Morton Trust Company either will not or cannot meet its obligations."

She got the cash.

At the same time, it was learned, she sold her furniture, oil paintings, sculpture, tapestries, and the other valuable possessions she had accumulated as the wife of Benjamin Wood, adding the money realized to the considerable sums resulting from her sale of stocks and bonds and the money withdrawn from banks and trust companies. Then she disappeared. The O'Brien firm understood that her withdrawal might not have been immediate. It was said that she and Mary and Emma traveled around the world. Whether they had or not, the three women did check into the Herald Square Hotel eventually.

In any case, O'Brien and his associates understood clearly enough that Ida Wood must have a rather formidable fortune remaining, and they concluded that the most important thing they could do for her at the moment was to protect her interests. They engaged the private detective firm of Noel Scaffa, and requested that guards be posted around Ida's room on a twenty-four-hour-a-day basis. The agency was told to instruct its men to prohibit any unauthorized person from entering the suite, and, as far as possible without intruding upon her, to keep an eye on Ida herself.

With that accomplished, the firm began to make arrangements for Mary Mayfield's funeral. Someone would have to consult Ida about the details, and Wentworth was given the job, since Ida seemed to have acquired a deep distrust of Morgan O'Brien, Jr., on the irrational ground that he was not his father. Wentworth was instructed to represent the firm in future dealings with Ida, to confer with her about the funeral, and to find out if he could whether Mary had left a will that might be offered for probate.

Blessed with a kindly manner and an abundant supply of tact, Wentworth began his task in a diplomatic manner by calling on Ida with a bunch of red roses in his hand. When she saw the flowers, she admitted him at once, and took the bouquet with obvious pleasure. For a moment one could almost see her again as the slim, dark beauty who had charmed so many men, and Ben Wood in particular.

Holding the roses in her hands, she looked at them for a long time. No doubt it was the first time in years she had seen fresh flowers. She buried her face in the petals, and stood, swaying slightly, for several minutes.

"I'm very glad you like them," Wentworth said gently.

A faint suggestion of a smile appeared on her faded lips. "I like flowers," she said quietly. "I used to have lots of flowers. I like them very much."

She found an old tin canister, ran some water in it, and arranged the roses, placing the container on the edge of a trunk. Then she sat down in her rocker, and favored Wentworth with a smile.

With this promising beginning, Wentworth chatted for some time, and appeared to be getting along well, although the conversation was hard going, inasmuch as he had to shout most of what he said. They discussed the funeral, and Ida agreed to the arrangements McDonnell had proposed. She also consented to have her sister's body removed from the suite, where it had lain for nearly two days, and taken to the funeral home to be prepared for burial.

Had Mary left a will? Wentworth inquired, as casually as he could.

"She did," Ida said, "and so did my daughter Emma."

"Was Emma's will ever probated?" Wentworth inquired.

Ida did not respond immediately, and the lawyer added, "Taken to court, I mean, so that her estate could be distributed?"

"I know, I know," Ida said testily. "No, it wasn't. No need for it. She left everything to me. So did my sister Mary."

"Do you have these wills here?" Wentworth persisted.

"Yes."

"Where are they?"

Ida jerked her head toward the bedroom door. "In there," she said. "That's where I keep them, and that's where they'll stay. We'll talk about them another time."

Wentworth sighed. Plainly there was no point in pursuing the matter at this first meeting, which had gone well enough anyway. He picked up his briefcase and hat.

"Thank you very much, Mrs. Wood," he said. "Perhaps I'll see you at Miss Mayfield's funeral tomorrow."

"Perhaps," Ida said, rocking slowly. "But I don't think I'll go."

She didn't. There were no mourners whatever, only the undertaker and four of his men, and the Reverend Samuel Gregor, who celebrated the funeral mass for Miss Mary in the Church of St. Francis of Assisi, at 135 West Thirty-first Street, where the casket was taken from McDonnell's funeral home. There were no cards, flowers, or telegrams. Ida was the only human remaining in the world who had been close enough to Mary to attend her funeral, and she remained at home. Father Gregor could not help thinking how much this stark funeral was like the other one at which he had officiated three years before, when Emma Wood had been buried from the same church. No one had attended that service either.

Faithfully, Father Gregor accompanied Mary Mayfield's casket to Calvary Cemetery in Queens, where he read the burial service, and dropped a few grains of earth on the coffin. Then he turned up his collar against the raw March wind, and hurried back to Manhattan.

Next day, and on successive days, Wentworth resumed his campaign to get Ida's confidence and cooperation. But she would not be wooed so easily. On some days she was a client, and on other days she consigned O'Brien, Boardman, Conboy, Memhard and Early and all their works to the devil, and refused to have anything to do with them. Wentworth tried to convince her that her securities and cash were not safe in the hotel rooms, and should be placed in a bank. She resolutely refused even to hear of it. He begged her to let someone in to clean up the two rooms, but she insisted that all maids were thieves and could not be trusted.

Then, unexpectedly, she relented one day, and permitted him to summon the floor maid to clean the parlor. "But she can't come in the bedroom," Ida added, fleeing there herself and locking the door. When the maid had gone, after an hour spent in trying to get the parlor tidy, she came out again.

Frequently Wentworth returned to the subject of the wills left by Mary and Emma, suggesting she give them to him so he could offer them for probate. Seemingly she would assent, giving him the documents from the old shoebox where she kept them. A moment later she would snatch them back. Wentworth persisted, gently and firmly, until one day she surrendered the wills.

"Take them to court, and do whatever you feel is necessary," she said. "I've had them long enough."

Next morning, when Wentworth reached his office, he was told that a woman had been trying to reach him from the Herald Square Hotel for an hour. It was the chambermaid who had cleaned the room the day before. Ida had instructed her to tell Wentworth that if he did not return the wills immediately, she would have him arrested.

Sighing, an act which had become customary in most of his dealings with Ida, Wentworth returned the wills, after which Ida locked herself in her bedroom, and did not come out for two days.

By this time two months had gone by since Miss Mary's funeral, and the situation at the Herald Square had reached a virtual impasse, in spite of everything Wentworth or anyone else could do. It was early May, and the O'Brien firm concluded that the best way to move the Ida Wood case ahead was to look for relatives who could protect Ida's interests. The path led directly to New Brighton, Staten Island, and the home of Otis F. Wood, a son of Fernando Wood, therefore a nephew of Ben. Presumably he was Ida's closest living relative.

With this discovery, the impasse was broken, but Ida herself was projected into a new and utterly distasteful period of her tangled life.

3

WHEN HE LEARNED about his aunt, Otis Wood was dumbfounded. "I thought she was dead," he told O'Brien. "I hadn't thought of her at all for a good many years. Let's see now, I can only remember seeing her once when I was a boy. I couldn't have been more than seven, and I can scarcely recall it. There was never any association between our families."

It was not surprising. The affairs of the Wood family were complicated far beyond the ordinary, because Fernando had been married several times, and there had been children by each wife. In this welter of relationships, Otis had never been able to keep track of his Uncle Benjamin and Aunt Ida. It was his belief, he told the lawyers, that Uncle Ben had at least one daughter, Emma, but he wasn't sure whether she was Aunt Ida's child, nor could he say whether Ida had had any sisters, brothers, cousins, or other relatives. Nevertheless, the attorneys suggested that he go to the Herald Square and talk with his Aunt Ida, hoping perhaps she would give him, as a member of the family, information she would not impart to them.

The attorneys also suggested that Otis be accompanied by Monsignor Michael J. Lavelle. On one of Wentworth's frustrating visits to Ida, she had mentioned Father Lavelle, as she called him, and expressed a desire to see him. "I knew him as a young curate in St. Patrick's Cathedral," she said, "and I met him occasionally at Judge O'Brien's home." When the Right Reverend Monsignor Michael J. Lavelle, then in his seventies, was told of Ida's request, he agreed to visit her, remarking that it was his hope he might persuade Ida to accept the care and comfort to which her years entitled her.

Accompanied by Monsignor Lavelle, Otis embarked on his first visit to his Aunt Ida.

It took some time for Ida to understand who Otis was when they confronted each other. It had been more than sixty years since she had seen him, and he was then a young boy; now he was an elderly man. As for Monsignor Lavelle, Ida refused to believe it was he. He was an old man, she complained, whereas the Father Lavelle she had known was young. When it was pointed out to her that more than forty years had elapsed since she last saw him, she reluctantly agreed that the years were probably responsible for the change in his physical appearance.

After a time, although the conversation was a difficult one, Otis did manage to ask some pertinent questions. Was Emma her only child? he inquired.

"My only one, my daughter by Benjamin Wood," Ida said positively.

"Didn't Uncle Ben have some other children?" Otis asked.

"Yes, but they were illegitimate," Ida said bluntly.

"Did you ever get to know them?"

Ida was positive about that, too. "No, they weren't any relation of mine. We never had anything to do with them."

While this conversation produced nothing very helpful to the lawyers, Otis was able to assist them in locating other members of the Wood family. He himself had three brothers, and he had heard that there might be children or grandchildren of Ben Wood by a previous marriage. Whether Ida had any blood relatives, no one knew, because nothing was known of her background before she met Ben.

Otis and some of the other Wood relatives returned later on to talk to Ida, but the visits were hardly successful. Sometimes Ida did not know, or pretended not to know, who they were. At other times she ignored them entirely. Convinced by this behavior that their aged relative was not entirely sane, the Woods asked the attorneys to have a psychiatrist examine her.

O'Brien called in two specialists, Dr. William Van Pelt Garretson, a neurologist and psychologist at Fifth Avenue Hospital; and Dr. Isaac J. Furman, Superintendent of the Manhattan State Hospital, on Ward's Island in New York. These psychiatrists, accompanied by Monsignor Lavelle and Otis Wood, undertook to examine Ida on July 10, 1931. Later, Dr. Garretson described their difficulties:

"We went through what I found out was the usual procedure of almost knocking down the door of Mrs. Wood's apartment. We had to kick on the door, and bang on it for a considerable time. Finally, Mrs. Wood opened the door, but then she would talk only to the chambermaid. After a while the maid got her to realize that Monsignor Lavelle was there to see her, and she let him in."

Having paved the way as diplomatically as possible, Monsignor Lavelle persuaded Ida to let the doctors enter. They chatted for a time until Ida, apparently regarding them as general practitioners, began to talk freely about the various ailments from which she was suffering. Her eyesight had been failing, she said, and she had been trying to restore it by rubbing Vaseline on her eyes. At times, she said, she was certain that her ears were growing to the top of her head, and that she could feel them there. She complained, too, that her fingernails were growing into the palms of her hands.

"Why haven't you called a doctor before?" one of the psychiatrists asked.

"I don't like doctors, and I don't like lawyers," Ida answered curtly.

But she went on talking, declaring with evident satisfaction that there were no members of her immediate family still living, nor could she think of any relatives who would still be alive. "I'm ninety-three years old," she said with pride, "and there's nobody left."

She talked about her past life with Ben and his newspaper, and spoke confidentially of how she saved her money from the Panic of 1907, and from the people who were after it, by cashing in everything and moving into the hotel. "We even registered from Philadelphia to fool them all," she said triumphantly, "and we did."

By this time the doctors had so won Ida's confidence that she took them on a tour of the suite, pointing out dusty trunks which she said contained rare silk, and yellowed cardboard boxes which she declared were filled with jewels. Alternately trusting and suspicious, she told the doctors with bitterness that now and then someone climbed in through the transom and rifled her treasures. Her husband's watch had been stolen, she said, and several other watches set with diamonds, as well as her own diamond necklace.

"But they haven't stolen my money," she concluded, on a new note of triumph. "You know, I have $385,000 right here, all in currency. But it's hidden, and they don't know where it is. Sometimes," she added ruefully, "*I* don't remember where it is."

That was enough to convince the doctors, if what had gone on before was not. Ida was obviously incapable of taking care of herself and her possessions, they told the Woods, and in spite of the private detectives who were living next door and watching her constantly, there was a danger she might be robbed, or that she might do some harm to herself.

Acting on this advice after consultation with the Woods, the O'Brien firm as attorneys for Otis Wood instituted a proceeding in the New York State Supreme Court to have Ida declared legally incompetent to handle her own affairs. If she were so declared, the law provided that the court must appoint a committee to protect her person and to manage her property and affairs. While this proceeding was pending, Supreme Court Justice William Harmon Black appointed a special guardian to protect Ida's interests in the proceeding.

The special guardian was Edward T. Corcoran, a clever, soft-spoken lawyer who had accompanied President Wilson to Europe as a member of the American delegation to the peace conference after World War I.

Corcoran was appointed on July 23, 1931, and next day, like the others in the case, he made a pilgrimage to the Herald Square Hotel to talk with Ida, and inform her, somehow, that a move was being made to have her declared incompetent. He presumed she would be completely ignorant about this legal move, but he was wrong. Ida knew what a special guardian does, and she appeared to be familiar with the meaning of an incompetency proceeding. Naturally, she was incensed by the idea that she was to be the subject of one.

"You're just trying to get my money," she cried, "but you never will."

Corcoran tried to explain that after the hearing the court would appoint someone to look after her and safeguard her possessions. Taking his courage in hand, he also showed her an affidavit Dr. Garretson had prepared which declared that she was suffering from "a paranoid state of mind in the condition of senile deterioration," and it would be dangerous to leave her alone. Hastily Corcoran added, before Ida could digest this opinion, that her property would be protected by law, and it was his function as special guardian to protect her rights in this proceeding. That pleased Ida. She smiled when Corcoran left, and asked him to come back as soon as he could.

Two weeks later Corcoran returned, with Dr. Garretson, and found Ida in a thoroughly trusting mood for once. She got out an old shoebox and showed them eleven certificates of Union Pacific preferred stock, and a $10,000 registered first-mortgage land grant Union Pacific bond. The certificates were for 1,020 shares of preferred stock, some in Ida's name, others in Mary's.

"I've got $285,000 in cash besides," Ida told them. "My sister drew it out of the bank when business was getting bad, and I'm glad she did."

"Where is this money?" Corcoran inquired.

"I'm sure I don't know," Ida shrugged. "Mary put it somewhere, and I've forgotten where."

A few minutes later she was talking about the money again, but this time she said it was $385,000.

"You just said $285,000," Corcoran reminded her, remembering, however, that she had previously stated it was $385,000.

"No, I didn't, I said $385,000," Ida told him tartly.

These were Ida's little surprises for that day, but she had others when Corcoran and Dr. Garretson came again. She showed them some coupons she had cut from bonds, and a bundle of negotiable first-mortgage Union Pacific bonds, worth more than $50,000.

"Do you have any more of these?" Corcoran asked.

Ida nodded and went into the bedroom. The two men could see her poking into a cardboard box next to her bed. She took out three frying pans, several cake tins, and some other kitchenware, then removed a bulky package.

"Untie it," she said briefly to Corcoran, handing him the package. He pulled the string and the package fell open. A $500 Lincoln gold note and a $100 bank note fluttered to the floor. The package slipped in Corcoran's nervous hands and $95,000 worth of Union Pacific bonds spilled out.

Corcoran was doing rapid addition in his head. There must be, he estimated, more than $200,000 in bonds in that suite, besides the cash Ida had talked about, whether $285,000 or $100,000 more. A man with a natural respect for large sums of money, Corcoran passed a trembling hand over his damp brow as he thought of the prospect before him.

"Look, Mrs. Wood," he implored. "You *must* let us put these bonds and certificates in a safe place."

That remark changed Ida's mood abruptly.

"I've got a safe place," she cried. With astonishing speed she gathered up the bonds and the two bills and dumped them back into the cardboard box. Then she threw the frying pans and the cake tins on top.

Corcoran was utterly frustrated. Under the law, he had no power to take possession of her bonds or money, even though he was Ida's special guardian. He could only urge that the detectives take extra precautions not to let any unauthorized person into the room.

Next night, however, he was startled out of a sound sleep by a call from one of the detectives. Ida was screaming for a doctor. At least she hasn't been robbed, Corcoran thought, as he hurried to the hotel, having meanwhile called a Dr. Van Ness at the McAlpin. But when the two men arrived in Ida's room, she was perfectly quiet.

"A doctor?" she asked mildly. "Why? I feel all right. No need for a doctor."

Although it was Corcoran who needed to be calmed, the doctor gave Ida some medicine Dr. Garretson had prescribed to relax her, and left. Corcoran stayed on. He wanted to find out, if he could, what it was that had upset Ida. Trusting once more, she was ready to tell him.

"I was counting my money," she said, motioning him to follow her into the bedroom. "See?"

Looking at her pillow, Corcoran saw a $500 bank note. On the floor beside the bed was a bundle of nine more $500 notes. The spectacle threw the lawyer into a new fit of frustration. His voice rose angrily in spite of himself.

"You mustn't leave all this money lying around," he protested.

"I know," Ida said calmly.

"Do you want me to take care of it for you?"

Corcoran was astonished anew by her answer: "Yes, take care of it for me."

Hoping he could accomplish the deed before Ida changed

her mind, he picked up the money carefully, called in the detective as witness, made out a receipt which he gave to Ida, placed the cash in an envelope, and put it in his pocket.

"I'll put the money in a safe-deposit box, and report it to the court tomorrow morning," he assured her.

Ida sat rocking calmly, apparently paying no attention, but as Corcoran was leaving she inquired suddenly: "When are they going to have my incompetency proceeding?"

"In a week or two," Corcoran answered.

"Good," Ida said with satisfaction. "By that time I'll have everything destroyed." But so far as is known, she did nothing to carry out her threat.

4

THE WHEELS OF THE LAW began to turn, and a legal storm gathered over Ida's head.

There were now two sets of Woods, both potential inheritors of Ida's undoubted fortune. Otis Wood and three other sons of Fernando, all New York businessmen, and a bevy of grandchildren—ten Woods in all—had joined together and were represented by the O'Brien law firm. As Ida's nephews and grandnephews, this faction contended they were her closest kin. The other faction consisted of Ben's descendants by his asserted first marriage to a Catherine Davidson. There were five of them, headed by Blanche Wood Shields. This faction contended its members were direct descendants—not collateral relatives, as were nephews or grandnephews—because they were allegedly the children of Ida's husband Ben by a previous marriage. If their contentions were upheld, it would mean that Otis and his group would have no right to share in Ida's fortune.

Despite their differences, both factions agreed that nothing whatever could be done unless Ida were declared incompetent, and a committee appointed to take care of her affairs. The appointment of Corcoran as special guardian had been a necessary step in the incompetency proceeding. Now the next step was the hearing, known in legal terms as an "inquisition before a sheriff's jury."

All those who were concerned with the fate of Ida Wood gathered in the Hall of Records at 31 Chambers Street in New York City on the morning of Tuesday, August 18, 1931. Nobody then knew, of course, that six years later, almost to the day, a hearing to determine Ida's identity would be held in the same building. Scores of lawyers and hundreds of claimants would engage in a massive duel in which the weapons were documents, records, and other evidence, with a million dollars at stake.

Even at the 1931 incompetency hearing, the participants were a formidable group. There was Harold Wentworth of the O'Brien firm, scheduled to be the first witness. Corcoran was there, in his function as special guardian to protect Ida's rights, and with him was John Walsh, one of the detectives who had been watching Ida. Stiff and uneasy in a freshly pressed blue suit and a scarlet tie was William Henry Grant, the hotel elevator operator and bellboy, who had probably seen more of Ida during the years of her seclusion than anyone else. Margaret Kilkenny, the chambermaid, was there too, blossoming unexpectedly in a light summer frock and flowered hat. Doctors Garretson and Furman were also present, as was a representative of the bank with which Ida had done business, and a transfer clerk from the Union Pacific Railroad. Then there were the various Woods, and lawyers from the two firms representing them. Everyone was present and accounted for but Ida. The doctors had said she was too ill to appear.

A determination of incompetency is no small matter, and is surrounded by special statutory safeguards. The Supreme

Court appointed James G. Donovan, an attorney, to preside as Special Commissioner at the trial required by the statute. Under the law, it is necessary that the sheriff's jury consist of not less than twelve nor more than twenty-four persons, and that at least twelve jurors must concur in a finding. In this instance, the attorneys agreed upon a jury of thirteen, who were duly sworn after being pronounced satisfactory by all the attorneys and the special guardian.

With these preliminaries disposed of, the proceedings were opened by David Asch, of the O'Brien firm, a short, forceful man, who summarized what he hoped to prove.

"This proceeding," he began, "is brought under the provisions of the law of this state which makes persons incompetent to manage themselves or their affairs, in consequence of lunacy, idiocy, or imbecility arising from old age or loss of memory, understanding or other causes, wards of the Supreme Court of the State of New York."

Asch went on to tell what was known of Ida Wood's background, which at that point consisted primarily of her life in the Herald Square Hotel up to the time when Miss Mary had died and left Ida "entirely alone and without anyone to look after her affairs." He declared that members of his firm had found Ida to be "practically blind, practically deaf, very weak, totally incapacitated from taking care of herself as she should be taken care of, and . . . left without any outside assistance of any sort whatsoever.

"Moreover," he went on, "she retained in her rooms a large amount of negotiable, valuable securities and money, the exact amount of which we have never been able to ascertain, which is open to anyone who might choose to enter these rooms and take advantage of her deafness, blindness, and weakness, and who may in any other way injure the old lady or take her property away from her."

The hearing then settled down to the subject of Ida's behavior. William Henry Grant told of what he knew about Ida over the past fourteen years. Margaret Kilkenny, the floor maid, followed him, and told of her futile attempts to clean the apartment, and of how, after Miss Mary died, Ida had sent for her frequently and asked her to open cans of evaporated milk with an icepick. Wentworth winced a little, ruefully, as Miss Kilkenny testified that when he had first come, Ida had "liked him very much. But later she said that Mr. Wentworth was not a lawyer at all; that he was just an office boy, and that she was sorry she had let him in."

"Did she say anything further about the members of our firm?" Asch inquired.

"She said that Judge O'Brien was a hypocrite."

Trying to keep his face straight, Judge Talley of the law firm of Talley & Lamb, attorneys for the Blanche Shields faction, could not resist the temptation. "I suppose she left you out?" he inquired blandly of Asch.

"I have never seen the lady, Judge," Asch replied seriously.

Miss Kilkenny went on to testify that Ida often got out the wills which Emma and Mary had left, and asked her to read them aloud. "I read them all through for her quite a few times," Miss Kilkenny said, "and she sat and listened. She never said anything until I was finished, and then she'd say, 'That's right. That's just the way it is.' "

Ida had also told the maid that she had a will of her own, but cautiously refrained from letting her so much as look at it, much less read it aloud.

Corcoran appeared on the stand, and told in some detail

how he had tried to get Ida to relinquish her property for safekeeping, and how she had seemed to have confidence in him, but would never accept his recommendations fully. The doctors followed him to the stand, and gave their diagnosis, on which they were agreed, that Ida was of unsound mind. Dr. Garretson, in passing, recounted another of Corcoran's many frustrations, on the day when he and the special guardian were talking to Ida in the parlor, and she had inquired suddenly if they would like a piece of pie. "It's in the other room," she said.

"That gave Mr. Corcoran an opportunity for the first time to enter the other room," Dr. Garretson testified, "and he went in to get the piece of pie and also because he desired to see what was in the room, in endeavoring to find out just what her valuables were. Immediately the old lady pushed me aside, and she said: 'What is he doing in there? He will have to come right out of there. What is he doing in there?' And then Mr. Corcoran came back without the pie, and he said he left the pie in there, and she left us and went back to look for it. Then we all three entered this secret chamber and that gave us an opportunity of getting an observation of all this untidiness," which he went on to describe.

"I concluded," the doctor summarized, "that she has a persecutory trend, which is significant of what we call a paranoid state of mind in the condition of senile deterioration. By reason of the condition that she is now in, for her own physical good, she should have supervision—medical supervision." He added that, in his opinion, Ida was not competent to manage herself, and that it was very dangerous to leave her alone. "She, with her poor vision, and her ideas of persecution—which keep her up, prowling about the house at night—might well set the house on fire, and then she might fall and kill herself." She could not be brought into court because she had a bad cardiac condition.

John J. DeWitt, an employee of the Fifth Avenue Bank, testified that he had known not only Ida, but both Emma and Mary. He had been a witness to the wills of Emma and Mary. He had also witnessed a will signed by Ida. What had become of that will, he had no idea; he had never seen it again after he had signed it as a witness.

Following him on the stand was John V. Hutcheon, a transfer clerk of the Union Pacific Railroad, who testified about the number of shares of stock in the company Ida held, and the number held by Mary, as well as the bonds both owned. The railroad had never had any address for the sisters except the Fifth Avenue Bank, where neither of them had been depositors for many years, consequently dividends for them were being held in the main office. No one had known where to deliver them.

The subsequent testimony turned from incompetency to the problem of Ida's property. This was germane to the proceeding because the amount of Ida's property requiring protection would determine the size of the bond to be furnished by her committee in the event she were declared incompetent.

Wentworth, the first witness, told the court he had been worried about the $285,000 or $385,000 as the case might be, which Ida insisted she had in her rooms but had misplaced somewhere. When she had changed her mind and intimated it might be in a safety-deposit box, he had circularized every company maintaining safe-deposit boxes in New York, and had turned up some new information. Ida, Mary and Emma, it appeared, had maintained a joint box in the Safe Deposit Company of New York, but had given it up in 1913. In December of that year, they had opened a safe-deposit box in the Lincoln Safe Deposit Company, on Third Avenue, but it had been discontinued in 1928. The money, then, must be elsewhere, presumably among her effects in the hotel.

Wentworth testified that there were three or four trunks in Ida's apartment, but said she would not admit there was anything in them but silk. He had, however, succeeded in turning up some other property.

The Surrogate's Court had issued an order on the application of the O'Brien law firm to conduct a search for the last will and testament of Mary E. Mayfield at the Manhattan Storage and Warehouse Company, where she had rented two storage rooms. "Acting under this order," Wentworth testified, "I went to the Manhattan Storage and Warehouse Company at Seventh Avenue and Fifty-second Street, accompanied by a representative of the State Tax Commission. There were two rooms rented in the name of Mary E. Mayfield and we had the locks sawed off the two rooms.

"In one room, known as 8D-10, there were six trunks, locked, two large wire hampers, locked, and a miscellaneous assortment of pictures and frames. The other room was known as 8D-24, and it contained eleven trunks, all locked, and various suitcases and satchels."

It is no part of an incompetency proceeding to determine the alleged incompetent's next of kin. This determination is normally made in an independent proceeding in the Surrogate's Court after the person's death. But Otis Wood had raised the question in the incompetency proceeding by asserting in one of the paragraphs of his petition that the persons entitled to inherit Ida's property in the event she died leaving no valid will were the children and grandchildren of Ben's brother Fernando, Ida's nephews and grandnephews by marriage.

This was immediately challenged by Mrs. Shields and her group, who contended in their answer to the petition that *they* were the heirs because they were the grandchildren and great-grandchildren of Ben by his wife Catherine Davidson, and therefore took precedence over the nephews and grandnephews who were collateral relatives.

Although the question of Ida's next of kin was not relevant to the incompetency proceeding, it was ever present in the courtroom. Obviously Ida had not long to live, and she was going to leave a fortune of undetermined size.

It was not yet known whether she had made a valid will. If she died without leaving such a will, the property would go to her next of kin. No one in the courtroom that day could have imagined what an immense and perplexing problem this determination would become.

Throughout the hearing the attorneys for each of the Wood factions argued the question, though they seemed to agree that an incompetency proceeding was no place for such an argument. Testimony was nevertheless taken from representatives of the two factions "for the record" because the Otis Wood petition and Mrs. Shields' answer had raised the question.

Otis Wood testified to his relationship to the family and what he believed were the facts about Ida. His father's brother, Benjamin Wood, had been married to Ida E. Mayfield, he said, and he considered Emma Wood as their child. He and his brothers "had always heard in the family that Uncle Ben had plenty of illegitimate children," he testified, but he did not know nor could he name any of these children, if they existed. Ida had told him, he said, that the only relatives she had were Fernando's children.

The suggestion implied in Otis's testimony—that Mrs. Shields was the descendant of one of Ben's illegitimate children—caused that lady to leap to her feet in rage and protest. It was several minutes before the hearing could be resumed. From that moment, Mrs. Shields became an implacable foe of Otis. When it was called to her attention later that Ida had made a similar suggestion, Mrs. Shields included Ida in her wrath, though continuing to lay claim to the fortune.

When Mrs. Shields took the stand, she testified that she was the daughter of Henry Wood, a son of Ben by his first wife, Catherine Davidson. Her father had two other children, she said: Gertrude, and Howard, who had died in 1925 leaving three children.

The testimony of the two Wood factions was a foreshadowing of things to come. Obviously there would be a contest among these Woods to determine who were Ida's closest relatives and therefore her inheritors. The province of the sheriff's jury, however, was to decide whether Ida was able to take care of her affairs and her person.

It did not take them long to agree. When the jurymen returned after a brief deliberation, the foreman said: "Mr. Commissioner, we find that Ida E. Wood is possessed of an estate consisting of at least $161,188, consisting of stocks and bonds and her personal property, from which she is in receipt of an annual income of $6,480. And we find from the evidence presented here that Ida E. Wood is a lunatic, and because of such infirmity, is unable to take care of herself or her affairs."

Thus, on September 22, 1931, Ida was adjudged incompetent. Was she "a lunatic," as the jury put it, in its unscientific way? I doubt it. As one who became thoroughly familiar with her case, I believe she knew what was going on during the period of her alleged incompetency. She disclosed only as much information as she wanted to, carrying on a game in which she gave various people different and conflicting information. True she was eccentric, and obviously infirm and unable to take care of herself. On those grounds the verdict of incompetency was justified, but insanity is another matter.

In any case, the law had declared her incompetent, and Otis Wood was named "Committee of her person and her property." That meant he was now responsible for Ida's welfare, physical and financial, and he was accountable to the court for whatever action he might take.

By this time Ida was becoming something of a celebrity. The incompetency proceeding had opened up the story to the newspapers, and the New York City press was having a journalistic field day. Reporters and photographers had descended on the Herald Square Hotel in droves, but the private detectives had temporarily held them at bay on the fifth floor. Nevertheless, the reporters had been able to find out a good deal about Ida by reading the record of the incompetency proceeding, and by interviewing people in the hotel, the lawyers already involved in the case, and several people still living who had known Ida.

The headlines on their stories ranged all the way from the *Times'* relatively dignified: "Rich Recluse Found in Dingy

Suite at Herald Square Hotel," to the *Daily News* proclamation: "Recluse Found Naked in Hotel Suite."

Piecing together the work of several reporters, the *Herald Tribune* gave its readers a vivid picture of Ida's past glory. "A belle from New Orleans," its story said, "Mrs. Wood swept across the social horizon of New York in the 60's and 70's with bright plumage and a fragile beauty that made her remarkable even in the parasol age.

"She danced with the late King Edward VII when he visited this country as the Prince of Wales and dined at the residence of her brother-in-law, the Mayor, in the family residence on the Bloomingdale Road. She was one of the belles who attended the ball given for the Prince at the Academy of Music."

The paper's reporters had found people who remembered when Ida, resplendent in plumes and lace, would drive up Fifth Avenue in her victoria about four o'clock every afternoon, attended by two liveried footmen, and call for Benjamin at the Manhattan Club, "the marble palace built by A. T. Stewart," as the paper called it.

"She was always on the dot," the *Herald Tribune* went on romantically, "and the amiable Mr. Wood would leave his comfortable armchair hastily and join her in the carriage. Sitting very straight beside him, with her fringed parasol tilted against the sun, she would ride along Fifth Avenue, the set of her small body the epitome of dignity. To this day, she speaks of the 60's and 70's as the golden era and compares the 'hideous manifestations' of progress with the leisurely beauty of Fifth Avenue, when every house stood back from the street and flowers bloomed along the pavement's edge."

Eventually patience and ingenuity were rewarded, and at least two reporters contrived to slip past the detectives and get a few words with Ida herself. They had discovered that she was keeping her door open for an hour or so every day, an inexplicable change of habit which gave them an opportunity they had not expected. In these hurried conversations, Ida had some sharp things to say on the subject of incompetency.

"They're trying to put me away," she told a *Times* reporter, "but they'll never do it. My broker was named Frank Work, and he was a very handsome man. I sold out everything before the panic [of 1907] struck. I did quite well, you know, and it seems very strange they should call me incompetent. I made money and I kept it. So many people whom everyone considers quite competent can't do that."

On another day she remarked testily to one of the *Herald Tribune*'s men: "I don't want anyone to take care of me. I can take care of myself." The reporter noted that as she talked (and somewhat belying her words) she appeared to be holding a small bundle of money.

Otis Wood carried out the responsibility given him by the court. He hired day and night nurses to stay with Ida, and asked them to make notes of everything she said and did. A doctor was retained to look in on her every day, and the detectives continued their watch.

That was as much as Ida would permit. For a month after the court proceeding, she resisted every other effort Otis made to take over the management of her affairs. Sometimes she refused to see him, locking herself in the bedroom. At other times she sat in her chair and dozed while he talked to her. She flatly refused to turn over any of her cash and securities.

Frustrated as everyone else had been, Otis decided that more drastic measures were necessary. He rented an identical suite of rooms on the fourth floor, directly under the apartment where Ida had lived so long, and on October 6, 1931, two nurses, a doctor, and two detectives removed Ida forcibly downstairs. The transfer was witnessed by representatives of both Wood factions, to see that nothing untoward was done.

Although the nurses and the doctor took every precaution to see that she was handled as gently as possible, Ida fought her removal from the suite which was so familiar. She had to be carried most of the way. "You're only doing this so you can go through my things and steal my money!" she cried, "but you'll never find anything. I've hidden it too carefully."

What might be in that incredible jumble of belongings on the fifth floor no one knew, but now another avenue to Ida's past had been opened—a past which was beginning to take on a more mysterious coloration with every day. The two Wood factions could hardly wait to explore that avenue. They hoped a pot of gold might be lying at the end of it.

5

As THE SEARCHERS—again with both Wood factions and their lawyers represented—began to plunge through the jungle in the fifth-floor suite, it appeared at first that Ida had, as she promised, hidden everything too carefully to be found, or else that her supposed wealth had been exaggerated. The first hour or so of searching produced only some old gold rings, a few brooches, and a silver bracelet.

Then they stumbled onto a gold mine. It was a crumbling, yellowed shoebox at the bottom of a pile of old newspapers and magazines, where a bundle in brown wrapping paper was opened to disclose no less than $247,000, most of it in $5,000 and $1,000 bills. That discovery sharpened the search to an exceedingly fine point. Everything within reach was searched with painstaking care, but no more rich lodes like the shoebox were uncovered.

There was, however, an astonishing and fascinating collection of other objects. Bundles tied with string and wire were opened hopefully and found to contain only old newspaper clippings, notebooks, magazines, excelsior, string, bits of cloth, and small pieces of wood, like children's blocks. Trunks in the two rooms were pried open to disclose dozens and dozens of old dresses, ball gowns, negligees, housecoats, bathrobes, sweaters, capes, and underwear, and hats of every description—feathered, furred, and beaded.

In one corner of the bedroom were carefully tied bundles of the *Daily News,* Ben Wood's newspaper. The papers were crumbling and flaking, but they were carefully marked, like everything else in the room, for future reference. At that point no one could be sure what might be valuable in establishing Ida's family background and therefore her possible heirs.

The searchers, naturally, gave special attention to the hundreds of letters strewn about the rooms, some tied carefully in bundles, others simply scattered or thrown into boxes containing kitchen utensils, or in the trunks, mixed with the dresses. There were even some lying on the bathroom floor.

At the moment no one bothered to read all the letters; there were far too many of them. But one caught Otis Wood's eye because of its signature, "Faithfully yours, Charles Dickens." Dated April 9, 1867, and addressed to Ben Wood, it read:

"Dear Sir: I have the pleasure of acknowledging the receipt of your letter dated the sixteenth of last month. I pledge myself in pursuance of my memorandum of agreement already given to Mrs. Attwood, to write the story referred to in that letter and yours, for the sum of one thousand pounds sterling; the manuscript to be ready for you the first of August at latest and to become yours on the consideration mentioned in my communication to Mrs. Attwood. I hope it will be ready for presentation through Brown, Shipley and Company the first of July."

Whether Dickens' promised story ever appeared in the *News* is not known, although he was writing at the time for other American newspapers. The New York *Ledger* paid him a thousand pounds for a single story. Ben Wood may well have been trying to repair in those post-Civil War years the severe damage done to his paper's reputation during the conflict.

To Otis Wood, plunging into the heterogeneous assortment of Ida's trunks, it was like "jumping back into another century," as he told *The New York Times* in an interview. In one trunk he found some jewelry and a splendid lace dress marked "Paris 1870." He believed it was the one Ida had worn to the ball for Empress Eugenie.

Meanwhile, Ida herself had found an unexpected ally in the press, whose reporters were much more willing to listen to her than to Otis. She talked to them at every opportunity, constantly reinforcing her charge that the Wood family was trying to put her away.

"I'm still young mentally," she told the man from the *World-Telegram,* "but they're going to try to put me in an institution. Well, I won't go. And if they try to take me out of here, you'll find that I'm not old physically, either."

What they could not supply in fact, the newspapers provided in fancy. It was reported that Ida was in a state of ignorance about everything that had happened in the world for the past twenty-odd years, and consequently had never heard a radio, or looked at a talking motion picture, or flown in an airplane. One reporter wrote that Ida had told him she knew he was lying when he said that people could actually fly through the air.

Otis Wood discounted most of these stories. Ida had known for some time about all these marvels, he said, but she wasn't the least bit interested in any of them. "We'd give her a radio, but she's so deaf she can't hear it," he said. "As for the movies, she couldn't see them if we took her, and in her condition, it's impossible to take her up in an airplane."

Ida was busy enough, it appeared, talking to reporters and doctors and lawyers and relatives. Following their instructions, the nurses were filling dozens of notebooks with everything she said. But on October 7, something occurred to break the routine. The nurse on duty in room 451, the new parlor where Ida spent most of her time now, noted that she appeared to be doing something to the back of her skirt—"hitching up," as she later described it. The nurse was curious, but, unwilling to annoy her charge unnecessarily, she waited to investigate until Ida lay down for a nap.

Gently patting the ancient lady's skirt, the nurse detected something that felt like a bundle underneath. Lifting the skirt cautiously, she discovered that Ida had a string around her waist from which was suspended a canvas and oilskin bag. She snipped it off with a pair of scissors, and, summoning one of the detectives to witness, she opened it on the table. A veritable flood of $10,000 bills spilled out.

"You count it," the nurse said. "I'm afraid."

The detective counted fifty bills—a total of $500,000. Added to the $247,000 in cash already discovered and the jewelry not yet appraised, Ida's fortune was now nearly a million dollars.

The revelation of this new bonanza caused a stir and commotion in the Wood camp. Notified at once, the parlor was filled with relatives and their lawyers before Ida had wakened from her sleep. Oddly enough, it was only then that the nurse happened to see a legal-appearing document protruding from the pocket of Ida's skirt. Taking it out, she handed it to one of the lawyers. It was Emma's will, bequeathing the sum of $3,000, on deposit in a bank, to Ida. Otis Wood took possession of it, to file it for probate next day.

Soon after, Ida woke up, and was told as gently as possible that the $500,000 had been found. To everyone's astonishment, she seemed unconcerned.

"It will be deposited in the bank so it will be safe and no one can steal it," Otis reassured her.

"All right," Ida said, nodding, "all right. Put it in the bank if you must. But what about the other money?"

"What other money?" Otis inquired.

"The other money I had upstairs," Ida answered. "It's gone, you know."

Otis was somewhat confused. "Well, we deposited the $247,000 you had up there, and you've got the receipt for it. That's perfectly safe."

"No, not that money," Ida said. "I mean the money somebody stole."

Otis was puzzled and alarmed. "Somebody stole some other money?"

"Yes, they did."

"How much was it?"

"It was a lot," Ida said. "It was more than a million dollars."

That was enough to set the searchers off again, in a state of some excitement. They returned to the fifth-floor apartment next day, reexamined everything they had looked at before, and searched exhaustively for things they might have missed. They explored the contents of the seven trunks in the rooms all over again, inspecting every garment in them, feeling the hems and linings to see whether the money might be hidden there. They pulled apart the two or three dozen shoes that were lying about. Every one of the large cardboard cartons in which Ida had kept everything from frying pans to lace fans was taken apart and the contents sorted and examined. At least five thousand pieces of soap, gathered from hotels all over the world, most of them still in their original paper wrappers, were examined with utmost care. Some were broken in pieces, to see if anything might be inside.

Canisters were explored, old jewel cases opened and the linings removed, books and magazines inspected, perfume and cologne bottles emptied of their contents and peered into. Yellowed, bedraggled corsets were sliced open, their slivers of whalebone removed and the sections of padding inspected. Nothing, however, was to be found in any of these possessions.

Then the searchers turned to the furniture. Every chair, table, bed, lamp, desk, and trunk in the two rooms was taken apart methodically. This search produced a ring and a piece of costume jewelry here and there, apparently long since forgotten, but nothing else of value.

A plumber took apart the old-fashioned radiators in the parlor and bedroom. He inspected the water closet, the toilet itself, and the traps in the drain. A carpenter went over every inch of the floor and the baseboards to find out whether any had ever been removed. The walls were tapped to find out if there were any unusual hollow spaces which might have been used as hiding places. Even the mattresses on which Ida and Mary had slept were sliced open. But not as much as a dollar bill was found anywhere.

The search turned next to the warehouse where Ida, Mary, and Emma had stored forty trunks. On a day in November,

1931, a delegation of relatives and lawyers from both Wood factions, accompanied by a covey of newspaper reporters, entered the huge Manhattan Storage Warehouse at Seventh Avenue and Fifty-second Street, and soon began opening trunks. It was a tremendous undertaking, and the search went on for several days, while the expedition's progress was recorded by the reporters in column after column of type.

What was found did nothing to reveal where Ida's second million had disappeared, but it shed further light on her life with Ben Wood, and on Ben's own life. Among the dusty portraits and photographs, for example, was a photo showing Ben as a Congressman in 1863, posed with fourteen other members of the House of Representatives. Lying beneath it was a framed copy of an ordinance passed by the State of Louisiana when it broke away from the Union. It was signed by all the members of the Louisiana legislature, and had apparently been presented to Ida's husband in grateful recognition of all he had done, or tried to do, for secession.

These and other pictorial relics were lying on top of the trunks. When it came to getting inside the trunks themselves, the searchers found themselves blocked again. They had come with huge batches of keys found in Ida's rooms, but only one or two of them turned out to be trunk keys. Locksmiths had to be brought in, who examined the situation and declared that the trunks had not been touched for so long that even if the keys had been the right ones, the locks were too rusty to respond. With the skill of their craft, the locksmiths sawed out most of the locks and opened the trunks.

Lying across the clothing in the first trunk lay a gold-headed ebony cane. An inscription on it disclosed that it had been presented to Ben's father, Benjamin Wood, Sr., by President James Monroe. This handsome trophy was flanked by three dozen pieces of old soap, yellow and shrunken, with labels so dark with age the printing could not be deciphered; and by several balls of string, rolls of wrapping paper, and several bolts of linen toweling.

Underneath this layer the searchers found bolts of silk from Bonnet et Cie., of Lyon, France, still in their original boxes; laces from Spain and Ireland; and pieces of Bohemian glass, which the labels proclaimed had been blown expressly for Ida.

The second trunk proved to be full of fashionable gowns from Fifth Avenue stores long since out of business. These dresses looked as though they had never been worn. Some were silk, trimmed with lace; others were satin and velvet, trimmed with fur. There were also evening capes of gold and silver material.

As trunk after trunk yielded up its secrets, the searchers found not money but soap, in even larger quantities than had been in the hotel apartment. There were cakes from the old Continental Hotel in Philadelphia, the Ocean House at Newport, the Windsor in Jacksonville, and the Leland at Narragansett Beach in Rhode Island.

The soap was distributed among more impressive mementos of proud moments in Ida's life. There were, for instance, various treasures taken home from the inaugural ball given for President Benjamin Harrison in 1889, which Ida and Ben had attended. And there were menus—dozens of them. One commemorated a dinner at the Fifth Avenue Hotel which Ida had given her husband on his seventieth birthday.

Another was a dinner given by the New York Press Club at the Holland House in 1892, whose guest list included all the city's noted editors of the day. Some of the menus were hand-painted, others fringed with silk, still others printed on pink satin.

Out of the trunks, too, came bundles of Ben and Ida's correspondence, sandwiched in with several score of daguerreotypes and pounds of crumbling business stationery of the *Daily News.*

A real and unexpected treasure turned up in a trunk full of old books. Ben Wood, it appeared, had been a bibliophile, possessed of a valuable collection. There was a six-volume Shakespeare, bound in calf, whose title page showed it had been printed in 1723 for Jacob Tonson in the Strand. It had a foreword (probably a facsimile) by Ben Jonson, and his inscription "to the memory of my favorite author." A plate in the book showed it to be a subscription set, printed for a hundred and fifty subscribers led by the Duke of St. Albans. The set had belonged orginally to George Arnold, one of the Gentlemen of His Majesty's Most Honorable Privy Chamber.

Besides this collector's item, there were others: several first editions of Edgar Allen Poe; a four-volume *Birds of America,* by Audubon; and similar valuable editions. By significant contrast, there was one book with Ida's name on the flyleaf: it was *Computation of Interest Table.*

Although there was no time at the moment to read them carefully, the searchers were fascinated by the bundles of correspondence between Ida and Ben. Many of these were notes, delivered by messenger, from Ben at the Manhattan Club or some gambling place, explaining why he would not be home until late, or until the following day. Ben adorned these explanations with expressions of undying love for Ida. The letters written from out of town while he was on business trips told how much he longed to be with her.

As the search came to its inconclusive end, with no further clues to the missing million, tension began to mount between the two Wood factions. Blanche Wood Shields and her group accused Otis Wood and his followers of hiring "expensive doctors" to care for Ida instead of having her sent to an institution. They accused Otis of dissipating Ida's fortune. Lawyers, detectives, doctors, and nurses were getting the money which should be preserved for the heirs.

The wrangling came to a climax one morning when Blanche Shields and her husband, accompanied by her sister Gertrude Wood and their attorney, knocked on the door of Room 451. When the nurse opened it, they pushed her aside and entered. Ida heard them coming, and, not recognizing them, she concluded they were hospital attendants come to take her away to an institution, and began to scream and cry hysterically.

Hearing the commotion, one of the detectives called Otis Wood, who hurried at once to the hotel. By the time he arrived, the nurses had succeeded in identifying Ida's visitors and they had seated themselves around her, shouting at each other and at the old lady. When Otis and his lawyer came in, Ida went into hysterics again.

Mrs. Shields undertook to explain that she and Miss Wood had come to look after her welfare. Ida answered that there was nothing wrong with her welfare, and she would be much better if everyone would leave her alone. At that point Mrs. Shields noticed what appeared to be black-and-blue marks on Ida's body, and a fresh scar on her upper lip that seemed to be the result of a burn. Mrs. Shields was indignant. She demanded to know whether Ida had been injured when she was forcibly removed from the upstairs suite. Otis said he thought not.

"On the day we moved her," he recalled, "she was sitting in her chair, the one she always sits in. Dr. Garretson said to her: 'You have to give up these rooms. The hotel wants them.' She said: 'I want to stay here. I'm happy here.'

"So they took a blanket—one of the detectives and the nurse—and went up to her. They wrapped it around her so she wouldn't be cold, like a comforter."

"Or like a straitjacket?" someone asked.

"Well, yes," Otis admitted, "if you want to put it that way. Then they lifted up the chair, and one of them held her feet, and she was carried out the door, down the hall and down the stairs. She screamed all the way, but she stopped when we were going downstairs, possibly because she was afraid she would be dropped down the steps if she didn't."

Mrs. Shields inspected the bruises, and when the nurse explained that they were the result of a blood condition, she merely looked skeptical.

"Where did she get that burn scar?" Mrs. Shields demanded.

"She smokes cigars," the nurse said calmly, "and one day she got the cigar turned around, and put the burning end into her mouth."

That answer effectively ended the questioning, although Mrs. Shields and her party announced themselves as unsatisfied. They told Otis Wood that they meant to apply to Supreme Court Justice Irwin Untermyer for a hearing on charges that Ida had been mistreated under his (Otis's) administration as the committee in charge of her. Otis only sighed, perhaps remembering how uncomplicated his life had been before his aunt and her fortune had been discovered. He asked the hotel management to send for locksmiths, and place heavy chains and safety locks on Ida's doors; then he went down to the lobby to confront the reporters who were waiting for him, having heard of Mrs. Shields's dramatic invasion.

Ida was settling down now, he assured them. "The excitement was very bad for her," he said. "She could only assume, with so many visitors coming in, that she was being taken to an institution. She fears that more than anything."

Otis went on to remark that he thought Ida had improved mentally and physically to some extent since she had been moved to cleaner rooms and prettied up a little by the nurses. "She's a curious mixture of sentiment and hard sense," he observed. "She wanted two things today: Her photograph folio of old pictures taken in the '50's and '60's, and a sight of her bankbook. We are, of course, letting her have both."

If Ida continued to improve, he went on, it might be possible to move her again, to "some high apartment with a southern exposure where she can live comfortably with some companions and, perhaps, a cat. She has been living all these years since 1907 on the north side of the hotel, and has hardly seen the sun. I want her to have sunshine, just as I want her to have good food and proper care. She will not be sent to a sanitarium as long as I have anything to do with it."

But with all that money in existence, and as much more still unaccounted for, if Ida's story of the missing million were true, there was little hope that the Recluse of Herald Square and her affairs would have the peace and quiet Otis had described. The story would not die in the newspapers and on the radio, and although there was a momentary lack of new developments in the case after Blanche Shields's invasion, this dearth hardly deterred the more imaginative writers and broadcasters.

One story widely circulated was that Ida had made a trip around the world carrying $700,000 in a paper bag tied to her wrist. Before they retired completely to the Herald Square, she and Mary and Emma were said to have visited France, England, Germany, Italy, and various areas of Asia, with Ida's valuable bundle in a bag strung on a string around her waist. In Africa, however, she somehow got the idea that any native who might want to rob her would look for just such a hiding place. "So I took the $700,000 I had with me," the papers quoted her, "and put it in a brown paper bag. Then I tied the bag to my wrist with some string. I went sight-seeing all over Africa with the money in the bag, and nobody ever suspected that I had anything of value in it. Besides, when I had the money on my wrist, I could feel it with my fingers."

When Otis and others asked her about this story, Ida sometimes denied it, and at other times not only confirmed it but added some colorful details of her own. But the next day, or the next hour, she might say, "Such rot and nonsense. Of course I never kept my money in a paper bag."

This inconsistency made the question of the missing million all the more baffling. The Woods were beginning to believe that it was an invention of Ida's, but on the other hand there was the nagging possibility that it might really exist, and they had somehow overlooked it. Having turned everything she owned inside out without success, they had no idea where to look next until someone wondered whether Ida might have slipped the money and perhaps other valuables into her sister Mary's coffin when she died.

Questioning of P. B. McDonnell, the undertaker, brought from him the startling admission that he had not embalmed Mary's body. Indeed, he had buried her in the clothes he found her in at the Herald Square after she died. A court order was immediately obtained for the exhumation of Mary's body, and Otis and Blanche witnessed the macabre proceeding of Mary's disinterment and the opening of her coffin. There was nothing in the coffin except the body of Miss Mary.

The second million, in fact, was never found, and there is no substantial evidence that it ever existed, although Ida went on insisting it did. She advised the searchers not to bother looking for any more of her jewelry. "I never had much, and you've found everything I have," she told Otis.

A month or two later, however, it was plain that she was only throwing them off the track. One day while Ida was asleep, the nurses on duty threw out three boxes of old, moldy crackers which Ida had kept close by her bed. Sitting down again after she had deposited the boxes in a large can outside in the corridor, the nurse had what she described later as "a very funny, itchy sensation." She got up, hurried down the corridor and retrieved the boxes. Ripped open and dissected, the first box held nothing but crackers. The second box, however, had a treasure nestled among the crumbs at the bottom: A stunning diamond and emerald necklace. There were only crackers in the third box.

Ida was strangely unperturbed when she was told the

necklace had been found. "Take good care of it," she remarked. "It cost Mr. Wood a great deal of money."

It must have, indeed, because it was later sold for $37,000, and it was only one of the many handsome pieces Ben Wood had lavished on his beautiful wife. The search had already turned up a diamond bar pin with three pendants and twenty-nine diamonds; two pairs of gold and diamond earrings, one with two 12-carat diamonds and the other with two 3.50-carat diamonds, and a solitaire diamond ring with a 5-carat diamond at its center. The prize of the collection was a gold and diamond necklace, with thirty-five graduated diamonds, whose aggregate weight was 118.50 carats.

When the news of these treasures was added to what had been reported before, and the wire services had circulated the story everywhere in the country, it was not hard to imagine that a host of persons would come forward as Ida's alleged relatives, claiming her estate. This was happening, in fact, while Ida still lived.

The fifteen Woods, divided into two factions, had thought at first that the contest would be confined to them, but to their dismay it appeared that there might be people extant with a direct blood relationship to Ida herself. As early as October, 1931, two people in New Orleans who had read about the case wrote to New York lawyers, giving their names as Lindsay W. Mayfield, manager of a grocery store there, and Earl Neville Mayfield, Lindsay's nephew. They had read with interest, they said, that Ida had given her name as Mayfield when she married Benjamin Wood, and they noted that the accounts of the wedding, reported in some detail by reporters who had searched the files for Ida's background, had described her as the daughter of Judge

Henry Mayfield, a wealthy sugar planter from New Orleans, and that on her mother's side she came of distinguished Scottish ancestry, a descendant of the Earls of Crawford. Her maternal grandfather, according to contemporary accounts of the wedding, was John Robert Crawford.

All this, wrote Lindsay Mayfield, convinced him that he and his nephew were Ida's only relatives because they, too, were related to Judge Henry Mayfield, and were descendants of the Earls of Crawford. Ida, he added, had been born and brought up in Catahoula Parish, Louisiana.

But Lindsay was no more alone than the Wood clan in his claims. Letters from Mayfields and those related to Mayfields began to pour in, some to attorneys, asking to be represented, others to Ida herself, who could not even read them in her nearly blind state. These letters suggested that the Mayfields and the Crawfords had pretty well populated the entire South, with extensions in the Southwest, the Mississippi Valley, and even the Pacific Coast. All the writers inquired solicitously about Ida's health, and volunteered to do anything in their power to help her. Louisiana, it seemed, was teeming with Mayfields, all of them descended from Judge Henry Mayfield, the New Orleans sugar planter. Crawfords were nearly as prevalent, and a good many of them were prepared to prove their ancestry to a branch of the Earls of Crawford.

One of these letter writers, whose family had strayed far away from Louisiana to Oregon, addressed Ida as "Dear Aunt Ida," and promised to come and take care of her. She was the "daughter of Lewis Mayfield," she said. The nurse who read the letter to Ida asked if she knew the writer.

"I never heard of her," Ida said forthrightly.

One of the oddest letters came from a law firm composed almost entirely of attorneys named Mayfield. These Mayfield lawyers said that their father, who had gone to California many years before, must be Ida's long-lost brother, although there was no indication at the time that Ida even had a brother, lost or otherwise.

All these claims were debated in the press, and there was considerable editorial speculation as to whether Ida had prepared a will, and if so, who would get the fortune. Some papers licked their editorial chops over the prospect that Ida might not leave a will, in which case the fight over the fortune would be spectacular. The possibilities in the case, and the personalities involved, were so fascinating that the papers could not let the story go. The tabloids ran Sunday features on what little was known about Ida's life and background. Even *The New York Times* carried an up-to-the-minute report almost every day on the state of Ida's affairs.

Meanwhile, the quarrel between the Wood factions, no matter what might become of the burgeoning Mayfield claims, was approaching a new climax. Mrs. Shields had carried out her threat of a petition to Justice Untermyer, demanding that Otis be removed as Ida's committee, and that she and her sister, Gertrude Wood, replace him. They contended that, as grandchildren of Ben Wood by his wife Catherine Davidson, they were more closely related to Ben than Otis, and Ben's other nephews or grandnephews.

Justice Untermyer denied this application. He was not at all sure, he said, just who was Ida's closest relative. There was a dispute on this point at every turn, he went on, and pointed out that although Mrs. Shields insisted that Ben Wood had been married to Catherine Davidson before he married Ida, Ida herself had told several visitors that she was "the first and only wife of Benjamin Wood." Justice Untermyer did take note of the fact that Ida's fortune had increased considerably since the first hearing, and so he increased Otis's bond from $225,000 to $1,000,000. It was filed immediately.

At the hearing granted to Mrs. Shields, Justice Untermyer had heard her complaint that her group were under instructions not to enter Ida's rooms, even with a court order, and they asked to be given permission to see her whenever they thought it necessary. The court ruled against that, too. Justice Untermyer observed that he would respect Dr. Garretson's insistence that Ida should have absolute quiet.

The Shieldses had other complaints. They said they had been "tricked" into being absent when the $500,000 was found on Ida's person, and that other searches had been conducted without their presence. The justice agreed that thereafter they would be permitted to be present at all searching parties.

At the hearing it was disclosed that Ida's expenses had risen considerably since Mary's death. Until then she had subsisted on a few dollars a day for food and room rent. Now her care and observation during the past seven months had become expensive, and bills were presented from doctors, nurses, and detectives. Justice Untermyer allowed some and cut others, but the total was still $22,000 for Ida's first seven months as a public figure.

Meanwhile, the object of this growing controversy, apparently revived considerably by all the attention she had been getting, sat rocking in her chair on the fourth floor of the Herald Square Hotel, smoking her black cigars on occasion, and rubbing Vaseline on her face and throat, trying to preserve the fine complexion that had been part of her beauty, and somewhat succeeding in the effort, too. Her face was still relatively smooth, certainly nothing like the wrinkled skin one would expect in a woman past ninety.

She rocked and talked with the nurses, sometimes bullying them, sometimes smiling and friendly. She had not long to live, and then the storm would break in earnest.

6

Ida Wood's last days in the Herald Square Hotel were a study in memory. Her wandering mind was sometimes in the past, sometimes in the present, but always alert, and the old habits of living were as strong as ever, even though her environment had changed.

She appreciated, for instance, the manner in which the nurses brought her food, serving it on a white tray with a flower or two in a slender vase, and placing it on a small table in front of her rocker. But often she pushed it away suspiciously.

"How much did this cost?" she would ask.

If the nurses named a figure over one dollar, Ida usually got up and went into the bedroom. "It's too much," she would say as she departed. "Take it back. I won't eat it."

The nurses soon learned to tell her that the meal had cost only twenty-five cents or so, and then she ate with enjoyment.

A few times, when the nurses weren't looking, Ida ran to a partly opened window and screamed pitifully down into the roar of the Herald Square traffic, "Help! Help! I'm a prisoner. Get me out of here!" No one in the street as much as looked up because she could not be heard, and when the nurses got her back in her rocker, Ida would laugh at them. "Frightened you, didn't I?" she chortled.

She had given up the effort to dress, and remained in her old, faded flannel nightgown, with a union suit underneath, and bedraggled slippers on her feet. If she were disturbed in the night, she would cry out: "I want a Democratic policeman. Get me a Democratic policeman. He'll help me get my money back." The nurses did not understand her request for a "Democratic policeman." Perhaps they imagined she was seeking political intervention or engaging in fantasy. They would later learn that she was referring to an interesting series of events in the administration of her brother-in-law, Mayor Fernando Wood.

Much of the time, Ida was lost in reminiscence, talking with the nurses, who dutifully recorded everything she said.

"I'm a Mayfield" she would tell them. "They used to spell it M-a-i-f-e-i-l-d in the old days, you know. I grew up in the city of New Orleans, a wonderful city."

On another night she declared: "I was married when I was fifteen years old, but I would have been sixteen in another month. I ran away from home to marry Ben. We got married in the Continental Hotel in Philadelphia by a Protestant minister, and then twelve years later we were married in the Roman Catholic Church. . . ."

Sometimes she was a child again. "I liked to keep my money with me when I was a little girl," she murmured, her dark eyes soft and glowing with the memory of it. "It always seemed so good to have money. I had an allowance of one cent a week to spend on candy and pencils."

One evening she asked Miss MacDonald, one of her night nurses, to add up the money that had been deposited for her. It came to nearly a million dollars, but when Ida was told the figure, she snorted—a snort that would have stirred anguish anew in the Wood factions, if they had heard it.

"That isn't half my money," she cried. There were a few minutes of thoughtful silence while Ida did sums in her head. "I think it's a million and a half dollars, and $87,000 more." She sighed and shook her head. "Oh, dear, I wish I could get my cousin Terence Fitzpatrick out in San Francisco to come here and straighten up my affairs."

Then she was off again. The nurses had no way of knowing, of course, whether what she said about her past was true or imaginary. "My mother had a very good education, you know. She spoke German, Spanish, and Italian, and she wanted me to be educated too, so she sent me to boarding school in New Orleans. My brothers never married. My poor brother Louis was drowned up in Massachusetts. He was like me; he was wild.

"It was very funny how I met my husband. He came to our house when I was fifteen. My brother and I were up in the peach tree. He said: 'Well, I want to see the girl who could climb that tree.' Then I had to come down in front of him. I knew then I'd marry that man."

Occasionally Ida sang in a cracked but true voice, half-keening an old Irish ballad called "Young Mary Came Wandering Home," beginning:

It was on one cold winter's night
  As the wind blew across the wild moor,
When Mary came wandering home with her babe,
  Till she came to her father's door. . . .

As the brief remission that had made Ida seem more tractable came to an end, her health failed, and she appeared to lapse into the less rational regions of her mind. A new nurse coming on duty in January, 1932, found her sitting in the rocker with her long white hair cascading down over her face, covering it completely. It was several nights before the nurse could see it at all.

Ida was a pathetic figure to the four nurses who attended her. With compassion they watched her rocking slowly, endlessly. The curvature in her spine made it difficult for her to get settled in bed, so that she would sit for as long as four days and nights in her chair, the only place where she was comfortable. Often, at two o'clock in the morning, she would ask for some bacon, which she loved dearly.

"She would be very careful to tell you that you must put it in the pan for about half a second, and then take it right off," one of the nurses recalled later. "One night I had it on for about five minutes, and she wouldn't touch it."

Ida's other early morning passion was for oyster stew, about which she was equally particular. She was specific about the order. It had to be a pint of stew with exactly twelve large oysters in it. One night when the bellboy had brought up the stew, the nurse signed for it and handed the dish to Ida with a professional clucking, "Now, you take it before it gets cold."

Ida was not to be hurried. "First I have to count the oysters," she said, and, putting her fingers into the stew, she did. There were only eleven.

"Are you quite sure there aren't twelve?" the nurse asked.

"No," Ida said firmly, "there are eleven, and I want twelve."

"All right, I'll call back downstairs again," the nurse promised. When the bellboy reappeared, she told him, "Look, I said to put twelve oysters in here. You'll have to take this back."

"I can't take it back," the boy protested. "Nobody's going to eat it now."

"Take it downstairs, and throw it out," the nurse said patiently, "and bring up a whole new lot of oyster stew, but be sure there are exactly twelve oysters in it."

When the new stew appeared, Ida put her hand in and counted again.

"Well, are there twelve now?" the nurse inquired.

"Yes," Ida admitted, and added grudgingly, "but they're not very big."

Sometimes violent, sometimes reminiscing endlessly and confusingly about her past, Ida seemed to withdraw more and more from a world which no longer held her interest. She knew that her money had been taken away from her—her precious money, which she had preserved and defended for so long. It did not matter that the taking had not only been legal, but essential for the safeguarding of her interests, nor did it matter that she had no further need of money at all. She clutched, forlornly, the five-dollar bill that had been left to her.

A dozen times during the day and night she would cry out, "Where is my five-dollar bill?"

"Look in your little black bag, and you'll probably find it there," the nurse would say calmly.

Ida's frantic fingers would scratch in the bag until they found the precious bill. "All right," she would say, settling back again. But an hour later she might cry out again in alarm, "Where's my five-dollar bill?" The bill was always where she had placed it, never to remove it again—in a black purse on her dresser, tucked in with a few small family pictures she treasured.

As she drifted into half-consciousness in the days just before her death, Ida fought an unfriendly world to the last. She battled any attempt to take her temperature, or to make her more comfortable. Her long and once beautiful hands at ninety-four had the strength of steel bars, as more than one of the nurses could testify. She had, they thought, the strongest hands any of them had ever seen. They were both astonished and frightened by the strength remaining in her frail, bent body. "She could have broken your wrist easily," one of them remarked.

Yet the nurses could not help feeling an outpouring of sympathy for her. "I had a tremendous pity for Mrs. Wood," one of the night nurses explained later. "I felt for the position she found herself in. And there was something about her I liked. She might battle you about taking medicine or her temperature or something else, but a minute later she'd be telling you all about her life again, and saying that you were a very nice girl. There was something nice about Mrs. Wood. There must have been, or she couldn't have got along the way she did with everybody. Even if she scratched me, I couldn't dislike her. I couldn't dislike Mrs. Wood, no matter what she did."

Early in March, Ida caught cold, and it developed into pneumonia. Dr. Brooks Vance, who was now her personal physician, did what he could to ease her pain as she gasped for breath, and clutched at the counterpane. Whenever she could shake off her lethargy, Ida would strike at his hand.

The two nurses had to hold her by the arms as the doctor injected a sedative.

The room in which she lay contrived somehow to be as depressing as the bedroom in the suite above—even without the mountains of junk. There was a chipped mahogany chest of drawers against one wall, with a floor lamp next to it. Ida did not like illumination, and so there was no light to brighten the plain black iron bed with brass trimmings in which she lay. The shades were drawn, and the old white lace curtains were pulled across them. The dark tan carpet was threadbare near the doors and beside the bed. Nearby, on a small brown table, stood the rusted and stained two-burner stove Ida had used for so long to prepare her frugal meals. She had refused to be parted from it, and had also demanded that the old-fashioned icebox with moldy green brass handles and a large, chipped enamel basin underneath to catch the water be brought down from upstairs. In the bedroom closet a few remnants of her once lavish wardrobe had been hung on hangers by the nurses.

On the night of March 11th, the two night nurses were certain Ida would not live until morning. Her breathing was rapid, and she was restless, moving back and forth on the pillows against which she had been propped. Dr. Vance ordered that she be placed in a sitting position to aid her breathing.

About five o'clock in the morning, Ida went into a deep coma. Except for her hard, fast breathing, she did not move. The day nurses reported at 7:30, and the night nurses told them their patient could not last the day. Later that morning Ida had a severe heart attack, and, as one of the nurses said later, "It was too much for the poor little old body to bear."

Shortly before 1:00 P.M., her breathing became more rapid and shallow; her pulse was so faint the nurse could scarcely feel it. "Call Dr. Vance," she told her companion. The doctor hurried from his office on East Fifty-fourth Street, and when he opened the door of 451 without knocking, he found Otis Wood already there. Before they could speak, one of the nurses came out of the bedroom.

"I'm sorry, Doctor," she said, "but it's all over. She died five minutes ago."

Thus the end came for Ida E. Wood. She had battled the world for nearly a century, until at last, as the nurse said later, "It just seemed that she let all the fight go out of her."

Dr. Vance applied his stethoscope to be certain, then he parted the long white hair that had again fallen over her face, and saw that her eyes were closed. He went into the living room and talked with Otis, who once more called on undertaker McDonnell for his services.

As she lay in her coffin in the shabby hotel room, a curious transformation took place in Ida. Something of her old, compelling beauty returned as she lay there, exciting wonder in those who came to pay their respects.

"You could see what an extraordinarily pretty woman she once was when you saw her lying there at peace with all the world," the younger O'Brien recalled later. "Her complexion, in spite of her age, was as creamy and pink and as unwrinkled as any I have ever seen. It was like tinted ivory. Her profile was like a lovely cameo."

When Doctor Vance got back to his office on the day Ida died, he sat down to make out the death certificate. Never did such a certificate so badly require the form statement which concluded it: "In issuing this transcript of Record, the Department of Health of the City of New York does not certify to the truth of the statements made thereon, as no inquiry as to the facts has been provided by law."

But the doctor put down what he knew, which was all anyone knew at that juncture. The cause of death was not difficult: "coronary occlusion, chronic fibrous myocarditis, cardiac failure and bronchopneumonia, with secondary contributions of arteriosclerosis and nephrosclerosis"—or, as the obituaries had said more succinctly of her husband, "old age and a complication of ailments."

On the basis of what Otis and the nurses had told him, Dr. Vance filled out the remaining vital statistics. Born: "U.S.A.," but he did not put down any city or town. "Lifelong resident of New York City." Name of father: "Thomas Henry Mayfield," birthplace "Ireland." Maiden name of mother: "Ann Mary Crawford," birthplace "Ireland."

At the moment of Ida's death it seemed to the expectant heirs that the major question to be settled was the distribution of her wealth, and it was true that the search for heirs would be ultimately necessary. But more crucial, as it turned out, was the question which became more important every day: Who *was* Ida Wood?

Some of the facts about her were already well known. Others had been searched out in old records. When they were put together, they made a portrait of the Ida Wood that New York knew—the public Ida Wood, so to speak. It was the picture she presented to the world, and the one the world believed, for the most part, until she died.

7

When Ida came to New York in 1857, she was nineteen and lovely enough to make a place for herself in the world without resorting to any more than the usual feminine wiles. She had never before been to the "Empire City," as it was then beginning to be called, and she must have viewed it with excitement and wonder. It was like a giant, noisy carnival. Five hundred thousand people surged through its streets, and to a stranger in town, it must have seemed that they were all bent on having a good time.

Night in New York was a jungle in 1857. Gaslights threw a yellow glare over Broadway until morning. The dull rumble of horse-drawn omnibuses and hackney coaches was never still. Bars, restaurants, and hotels were doing a roaring business, and a new word had been coined to describe the men who made them prosperous. The word was "millionaire."

Ida would have been less than human if she had not explored the city thoroughly, or as thoroughly as a young girl alone could do. Presumably she went to Barnum's Museum, at Broadway and Ann Street, just south of City Hall, to see the congress of freaks. On the way, and crossing tumultuous Broadway traffic at her peril, she passed through quiet West

Side streets of new brownstones, marking an era that was just beginning. No doubt she regarded with awe the celebrated Astor House, on Broadway at Barclay, and the great white marble facade of the new St. Nicholas Hotel on Broadway at Broome, which was said to have cost more than a million dollars.

It is unlikely she had enough money to shop in A. T. Stewart's magnificent department store, whose six white marble stories took up the whole block on the east side of Broadway, between Chambers and Reade Streets. Nor could she have seen much of New York after dark in those first few weeks after her arrival. There were few parts of the city that would have been safe at night for any girl alone, much less one as beautiful as Ida. The East Side, from the Battery to the slums of Goat Hill, where Grand Central Station now rises, was a teeming slum.

What Ida did for a living, where she lived, who her friends were or whether she had any friends at all, no one can be certain.

We found among Ida's effects a faded, ornate and sentimental valentine dated February 14, 1857. The verse it carried was an acrostic—the first letter of each line was omitted, and the omitted letters reading downward spelled out the words, "DEAREST IDA MAYFIELD." The full text of the valentine was as follows:

> ear Ida, with the lovely eyes,
> ntrancing all on whom they fall,
> nd beauteous as the heavenly night
> adiant with stars; Oh may I call
> ach fond look, which they give my own?
> uch happiness would make me glad,

he thought would thrill through all my soul,
ntenser joy, soul never had.
ark as thy raven tresses, glowing,
shadow on my heart would fall,
ad'ning my brain, and 'ver me throwing
gloom, as black as funeral pall,
our love should any other claim,
or 'tis to me, Life, Hope, Joy, All!
da, then hear me! Grant my lover's prayer
nd every fear and bid Hope's rain-bow shine!
oad me not down with heavy black despair,
estroy each doubt, and be mine, only mine.

Feb 14th 1857
St. Valentine's Day

Our extensive investigation into the circumstances under which Ida obtained the valentine was not fruitful. We could not determine whether the "dearest Ida Mayfield" in the valentine was our Ida. While the valentine was dated 1857, we had no way of knowing that Ida then possessed it. The quality and ornateness of the paper on which it was written led us to believe it could be purchased only in a big city, like New York.

There was purpose in Ida's coming to the city. She had not drifted there merely looking for work, as so many restless girls and ambitious young men were doing in those days. Her purpose was to make a place for herself—a prominent place. She was poor and a nobody, but she had studied how to be a lady, as it proved, and she meant to be one, rich and respectable and admired in society. Ida's sensible, direct mind told her there was only one way to achieve such eminence, and that was to marry into it. She cast about for a rich man.

No one is certain how she met Benjamin Wood. Certainly it was not the fanciful girl-in-a-Southern-tree story she told the nurses in the Herald Square Hotel. Nor was it any of the other versions she provided. In one of these she said she met Ben when she was only fifteen, under circumstances not further disclosed, married him in a Philadelphia hotel, against the advice of her friends who thought he was too old for her, and lived happily ever after.

Ida would never have met Benjamin Wood in the ordinary course of events. He was then thirty-seven years old, a successful young businessman, whose business activities were deeply involved with his brother Fernando's political organization. Fernando was the mayor of New York, one of its worst, but his position led him into the gilded society of the city, and Benjamin followed him into those circles.

The evidence strongly suggests that Ida, a girl of extraordinary resourcefulness, took a direct route to Ben's heart, after hearing and reading of his exploits as a young man-about-town. In her effects, after her death, there was found a letter, faded and torn, but written on what would once have passed for personal blue notepaper. It was a letter as direct as Ida always was, and it read, under the dateline New York, May 28, 1857:

"Mr. Wood—Sir Having heard of you often, I venture to address you from hearing a young lady one of your *'former loves'* speak of you. She says you are fond of 'new faces.' I fancy that as I am *new* in the city and in 'affairs de coeur' that I might contract an agreeable intimacy with you; of as long duration as you saw fit to have it. I believe that I am not *extremely* bad looking, nor disagreeable. Perhaps not quite as handsome as the lady with you at present, but I *know* a little more, and there is an old saying —'Knowledge is power.' If you would wish an interview address a letter to No. (excised) Broadway P O New York stating where and what time we may meet. Yours truly. . . ."

The letter was signed *"Nellie,"* with something in parentheses after it carefully cut out, as was the Broadway P.O. number. Someone long after the fact, apparently—Ida herself, perhaps—wanted to cover up the damning details in this unabashed letter, particularly "Nellie's" real name, presumably in the parenthesis. But the handwriting was Ida's, the letter was found in her private papers, and her mother sometimes referred to her as Nellie.

Taken in the context of New York life and Ida's own incredible story, it is a letter that shows more of her indomitable will than it does of any intended immorality. As a sales letter, it produced immediate results. Ida and Ben met, and whatever the motivation on either side, they fell in love—or at least Ben did.

They must have been a handsome couple. Ben was a tall, vigorous, commanding man, with a mane of black hair, a black moustache and bold, fierce eyes. Ida was a slight, dark girl with a fine figure, long dark hair, an oval face with high cheekbones, and extraordinary eyes. Her manner was direct and elegant. She spoke in a soft, cultured voice in which there was no trace of an accent derived from the Louisiana plantations of the Mayfields.

From the time of their first meeting until their official, recorded marriage ten years later in 1867, the record is confusing, perplexing, and full of contradictions that have never been resolved. It is a decade in their private lives which is hidden and hard to explain, although in those turbulent war years the details of Benjamin Wood's public life could hardly have been more widely known.

Presumably their first meeting was in the Continental Hotel in Philadelphia. Whether Ida met him there after her inviting letter, and became his mistress for the next ten years because he may have been already married, or whether they had met before and were married secretly at this out-of-town hotel to confound Wood's enemies, is a question impossible to determine.

At this juncture in their joint fortunes, Ben's private life was as mysterious as Ida's. It seems he had a wife, Catherine, who had died in 1850 at their Williamsburg, Brooklyn, home. The census of 1860 listed him as living with his two sons at Manhasset, Long Island. At the same address there was listed a Delia Wood and her parents, people named Bowers.

Who was Delia Wood? No one knows; no one ever found out. She next appears in what is assuredly one of the most baffling episodes in the entire perplexing saga of Ida Wood. On August 19, 1867, in the pages of the New York *Daily News,* a paper then owned and published by Ben which he had acquired six years earlier, there appeared a death notice of Delia Wood, wife of the Honorable Benjamin Wood.

Perhaps the notice was inspired by some of the numerous enemies of Ben or his brother Fernando to cause either or both of them embarrassment. Or could this have been a clever device of Ida's to induce Ben to marry her in a church ceremony? It is not impossible. In any case, that was the result, although next day the *Daily News* printed an indignant denial of the death notice's authenticity. Everyone knew, the paper said, that Mr. and Mrs. Benjamin Wood (meaning Ben and Ida) lived on West Fifty-fourth Street, and were at that moment absent from the city. (They were, in fact, summering in Newport, along with the rest of New York society.) Nevertheless, two months later Ben and Ida were married at the Paulist Church on Fifty-ninth Street at Columbus Avenue in New York City. This marriage in the Catholic Church settled the relationship between Ida and Ben, and deprived his enemies of any basis for further gossip concerning Ben's private life.

Ida had asserted in the course of her reminiscing at the Herald Square, it will be recalled, that she had been married by a Protestant minister in Philadelphia in 1857. The Catholic religious ceremony in 1867 was presumably for the purpose of restoring her as a communicant in the Catholic Church.

On the other hand, there were nagging questions about such an explanation which were never resolved. Did Delia Wood's death in Manhasset, where she had been living with Ben until he met Ida, leave him free to marry—presuming the death notice identifying Delia as Ben's wife was authentic? The suspicion is strong that Delia was Ben's wife after the death in 1850 of Catherine, whom he had married in 1846; that he lived in the same house with her and her parents in Manhasset, and went on maintaining them there after Ida became either his mistress or his wife in Philadelphia. We were unable to find any evidence of a Philadelphia marriage in 1857, and came to believe that it was as a mistress, not as a wife, that Ida lived with Ben from 1857 until their authenticated marriage ten years later.

Ida, in fact, our investigation disclosed, was using the name Harvey in 1859. Silver was found among her effects bearing the letter "H," and the trademark evidence on it indicated that it was bought that year. The silver consisted of six forks, six teaspoons, and six tablespoons. By something that must have been more than coincidence, Benjamin Wood bought from Tiffany & Co., in 1859, that exact amount of silver, minus one tablespoon. If they were secretly married, why did Ida have this silver marked with an "H," presumably for Harvey, the name under which she was living at the time?

In 1864, Ida, using the name Ida Harvey, purchased a house at 213 West Fifty-fourth Street. As part of the transaction she executed a purchase money mortgage for $5,000. Ben witnessed her signature to the mortgage instrument. Undoubtedly he also furnished the money for purchasing the house. Two years later the census records her as living in that house as Mrs. Benjamin Wood, the first time she appears under that name. Ben, meanwhile, was listed by the census as living at Manhasset, Long Island, until 1866, when he too gave the Fifty-fourth Street address as his residence. In all those years Delia, too, presumably lived in Manhasset with her parents and Ben's children by his first wife. Was she known by her maiden name, Bowers? Ben called her that later. Or was she Delia Wood? That was how the census listed her, on information supposedly supplied by Delia herself, if not by Ben. Ben repeatedly assured Ida he had never married Delia, and it may be true, but still it is hard to account for her presence in his home, with her parents, on any other basis.

One thing is certain. Whether Ida was ever really Mrs. Harvey, and there is not the slightest evidence that she ever had a husband named Harvey, and whether Delia Bowers or Delia Wood was ever Mrs. Wood, Ida and Ben were inseparable from the moment they met. It was true love. Ben later wrote to a friend that she came to him as "a noble, artless, beautiful and virtuous girl," something "I had almost despaired of finding." She must have been an extremely skillful actress as well, because Ida turned out to be one of the most artful women of her time. But then, Ben was richly endowed with that quality himself.

The evidence suggests that from 1857 to 1867 they moved about the city openly, and that in 1864 they began to live together under the same roof on Fifty-fourth Street. As we later learned, correspondence addressed to her there concerned her brother, who was then in a boys' school, the House of the Angel Guardian, in Jamaica Plain, Massachusetts.

Ida and Ben did not live long on Fifty-fourth Street. They sold the house after their ceremonial church marriage, in a transaction that added a further complication to Ida's tangled web of identities. When the house was sold in November, a month after the wedding, Ida's sister Mary had to appear to furnish the legal assurance that Ida Harvey, who had bought the house, and Ida E. Wood, who was selling it, were one and the same person. Miss Mary signed herself Mary E. Walsh. A month before, she had signed the marriage certificate as a witness for her sister as Mary E. Walsh Mayfield.

The wedding was the climax of a stormy decade for the lovers, whether married or not—stormy not only in their troubled private lives, but in Ben's public life as a newspaper publisher, in which for a time he was a public enemy in the eyes of the Federal government. Since he was also cordially hated by a good many responsible and influential people in New York City, it is hard to explain why he publicly appeared with Ida in those days, when she was known as Mrs. Harvey.

But appear they did, whatever the unresolved matrimonial tangle may have been, stepping boldly into the social brilliance and turbulent political atmosphere of a New York gripped in the crisis of the Civil War.

8

IDA'S MEMORABLE DANCE with the Prince of Wales on his visit to the city in 1860 was a proof of Ben's influence, or his brother's, because only a select few were chosen for an honor coveted by every society woman in New York. It was the first time royalty had ever visited the city, and the excitement was intense. The Prince was not only royalty. He was nineteen, slim and handsome, with a reputation for frivolity and an eye for the ladies.

Old Peter Cooper, the distinguished merchant, would have preferred to give a banquet for the Prince, on the ground that it would be more dignified, but his Highness's representatives let it be known that the Prince, who would be traveling in America under the discreet incognito of Baron Renfrew, would much prefer a ball. He was bored to distraction with banquets and speeches.

The ball became the most exclusive event New York society had ever seen. The intrigue, the humiliating maneuvers to get invitations were hardly inspiring, and even worse was the feminine competition to get on the Prince's dancing list. Old friendships were broken, marriages threatened, unlikely alliances formed.

On a bright October afternoon, the Prince arrived and was

conveyed up Broadway from Bowling Green to the Fifth Avenue Hotel through a tumultuous throng of three hundred thousand people. He stopped long enough for the usual ceremony at City Hall. By the time his open carriage, drawn by six white horses, reached the hotel, it was dusk. The Fire Department gave him a torchlight parade that night, and the following morning Mayor Wood entertained him at breakfast at the mayoral house, Wood Lawn, out in the country at Broadway and Seventy-seventh Street. Ben and Ida may well have been at the breakfast. Ben was listed in the newspapers as a guest, but there was no mention of a Mrs. Harvey, as Ida was then apparently known.

Later in the day the Prince was taken to see the sights of New York—the Deaf and Dumb Asylum, New York University, Cooper Institute, the Astor Library. But this was only a perfunctory preliminary to the grand event of his visit, the ball, which was to be held in the Academy of Music on Fourteenth Street.

The baroque interior of the Academy was jammed to the doors, and the manners on display were not what might have been expected. The Duke of Newcastle observed, with well-bred distaste, that the way the crowd of young ladies surged and pressed about the Prince was "not in strict accordance with good breeding." No word of complaint was heard from the Prince, however, on that score. He danced with many of them, nearly all the young unmarried belles in town, and with the wives of the most prominent men. He must have been impressed by Ida's beauty, which added further glamour to an occasion already so breathtaking that the guests could never forget it. Dancing with the Prince lived in Ida's memory for more than seventy years.

How different, less than a year later, in 1861, must have been her meeting with Abraham Lincoln. By that time Ben had bought the *Daily News,* with the help of Fernando, and the nation stood in the shadow of civil war. Lincoln paused in New York on his way from Springfield to Washington as President-elect. His confrontation with Fernando Wood was a strained and painful occasion, as Carl Sandburg makes clear in his description of the event.

New York at that moment, says Sandburg in his Lincoln biography, was a place where "Mayor Fernando Wood had declared that New York should establish itself as a Free City, separate from the Union, and become sovereign in itself like the seceded States of the South, thereby holding its trade and continuing uninterrupted intercourse with every section of the country."

The city, Sandburg went on, was also a place "where the Mayor and his brother Ben owned the New York *Daily News,* openly advocated the rights of the Confederate States and covertly urged secession of New York City. . . ."

Ida's meeting with Lincoln could hardly have been the social occasion her fading memory recalled in her disjointed mutterings at the Herald Square Hotel seventy years later. His arrival was in sharp, almost sinister, contrast to the Prince of Wales's triumphal entry. Lincoln rode from the Hudson River Railroad Depot at Thirtieth Street and Ninth Avenue at the head of a procession of thirty carriages, his own barouche the same one which had held the Prince's royal person. But on the way to the Astor House, where he was to stay, there were no roaring throngs to greet him. The crowd was very large, and it was curious, but it was comparatively silent.

Part of the reason for this strange quiet was the antipathy toward Lincoln stirred up by Ben Wood's *Daily News*. It was going to be an unpopular war in New York, and even then Lincoln's views were being savagely attacked in a city which was predominantly on the side of the South. The crowd gathered to watch Lincoln's arrival was almost entirely male; the women did not turn out. Most of the estimated hundred thousand, the fourth largest crowd in the city's history, were gathered around the Astor, held in check by five hundred policemen.

Next morning Lincoln met his enemy, Mayor Wood, in the Governor's Room of City Hall. The place was filled with aldermen and the press. Wood never addressed his visitor as "Mr. President," but always as "Mr. Lincoln." He described New York as "sorely afflicted," with "all her material interests paralyzed," her "commercial greatness endangered." He hoped Lincoln would be able to do something about it by pursuing "peaceful and conciliatory" tactics with the South.

Lincoln, in reply, remarked frankly upon "the large majority" in New York who were not with him. But then, while Wood regarded him with a penetrating gaze which never wavered from the moment he confronted Lincoln, and which Lincoln did not return, the President seemed to speak beyond him to the whole country as he declared: "This Union shall never be abandoned, unless the possibility of its existence shall cease to exist without the necessity of throwing passengers and cargo overboard. So long, then, as it is possible that the prosperity and liberties of this people can be preserved within this Union, it shall be my purpose at all times to preserve it. . . ."

After the ceremony, Lincoln shook hands for two hours at

City Hall, and resumed these greetings later in the afternoon at a formal reception. Ben and Ida were no doubt in one of those lines filing past the President. That night they may have gone to the Academy of Music, where the President was taken to hear a performance of Verdi's *Un Ballo in Maschera.* If not, they might have been at the Astor House, where Mrs. Lincoln was holding a reception which could only have been described as a social failure. Only a hundred people came, out of several hundred invited, and Mrs. August Belmont, the queen bee, took pains to deny publicly next day the reports in the papers that she had attended.

Ben had stepped into the violent journalism of the time as though he had been made for it, notwithstanding that there was little in his educational background to indicate he might have the talent. Born in Shelbyville, Kentucky, on October 13, 1820, he had enjoyed no more than a common school education. As the *Times* said in its obituary, he was self-supporting "when but a stripling." How he supported himself is not exactly clear. Sometimes he shipped as supercargo on vessels bound for the Antilles and Central America. Once he worked in the bayous of Louisiana as a moss gatherer. Later, he came to New York and settled down to what was euphemistically described as a "mercantile career." That appeared to consist principally of profiting from the deals, legal and otherwise, which the Mayor was able to toss his way, and from the gambling enterprises which were prospering both of them.

By 1861, however, Ben was started on his real career as publisher and politician. He had been elected to Congress from the Third District, and he had bought the *Daily News,* the organ of his brother's administration, founded in 1855 by W. Drake Parsons. The paper had begun as a one-cent morning paper of four pages, and had done so well in six years that it had increased its size to eight pages and its price to two cents. Its columns were soon filled with radical pro-slavery talk, and with fiercely partisan support for Fernando Wood and all his many works.

In the pages of the *Daily News,* New Yorkers read for the first time the mayor's astonishing proposition that the city should secede from the Union. It was a proposal consistent with the bitter attacks on Lincoln which Ben and his editors wrote. Ben had just been elected to Congress in 1861 when these attacks reached a point that the government could not ignore. On orders from Washington, the New York post-master refused to accept the paper for mailing, and Ben had to use Railway Express to get his propaganda into other cities. The government put a stop to that, too, when the evasion was discovered. Detectives were planted on every express train leaving New York, and when they spotted bundles of the *Daily News,* the papers were seized. There was little Ben could do except to suspend publication, because an important part of the paper's revenue was from out-of-state circulation.

When publication was resumed nearly eighteen months later, it had switched from a morning to an evening newspaper, and increased mightily in virulence, as the passions of the war reached a climax. The private war of Ben Wood and his brother against Lincoln and the Union reached its peak in 1864, the darkest year. An 1863 editorial in the *News,* published just before the Battle of Gettysburg, had helped to precipitate the mass insanity of the draft riots in New York, when lawless mobs captured the city, and fought with police and Federal troops brought in from the battlefields of Pennsylvania. In five days of terror, more than two thousand men and women were killed, and eight thousand more were injured; the property damage was estimated at more than five million dollars.

It was about this time that the paper acquired as editor a man named Phineas C. Wright, who had been national head of a secret, subversive organization known as the Sons of Liberty, dedicated to the overthrow of Lincoln and his government. When Wright left for New York, he was succeeded by the notorious Clement L. Vallandigham, the Copperhead editor who was such a thorn in Lincoln's side.

"Copperhead" was a word which had come into general use to characterize Northerners who were pro-Southern, particularly the Democrats who fought the Lincoln Administration sometimes beyond the edge of treason. Although the Copperheads closely associated themselves with the Democratic Party, they were actually only a small and virulent element in the party's total structure, and did not represent the views of its responsible members or national policy makers.

During his first day on the job, in January, 1864, Phineas Wright composed a circular letter which he sent out to Sons of Liberty leaders everywhere in the North. It was written boldly on the letterhead of the *Daily News,* and advised the Copperhead fanatics that the paper was dedicated to fighting the Lincoln Administration's "usurpation of power," and that it would henceforth be "our" newspaper. The letter ended with a plea for subscribers.

On other occasions the paper talked about "the emptiness and folly of this war against brethren," and until the last gun was fired, it continued to insist that Union victories were frauds, and the South would never be defeated. "You may conquer, but you can never subdue them," Ben said.

The publisher's violent attacks on Lincoln and the Administration kept him and the paper in constant trouble. At the time of its suspension, the *Daily News* had been named in a grand jury presentment, along with three other papers, charging disloyal conduct. Now, in 1864, Congress itself moved against its disloyal member, Benjamin Wood. Formal charges were brought against him in the House for disloyal statements he had made on the floor, in which he had repeated some of the material in his paper. These charges were referred to the Judiciary Committee. It appears that the Committee failed, nevertheless, to take any formal action.

The publicity was enough to discourage another term immediately, however, and Ben came home from Washington in March, 1865. But his political appetite was not yet satisfied. He ran for the New York State Senate in 1866, and was elected for a term. Years later, in 1880, he ran again for Congress, this time from the Fifth District, was elected, and served another term.

Fernando's political career was also turbulent, and Ida was undoubtedly more than a casual observer of his political ups and downs. He was Mayor of New York City from 1855 to 1858, and again from 1860 to 1862. Fernando feuded not only with Lincoln on Civil War policy, but with the Republicans at Albany on state-city relations. The Republicans who controlled the state legislature retaliated by reducing Fernando's second term from two years to one, and by establishing a state-controlled metropolitan police force to supersede the city's police. Fernando responded by refusing to disband the municipal police force, whose members became known as "Democratic policemen."

This was why Ida, in her cries for help when she was watched over by nurses in her last days at the Herald Square Hotel, pleaded: "Get me a Democratic policeman, I want a Democratic policeman."

While the constitutional issue over the state's action was fought in the courts, the two warring police forces battled for power in the streets. A bloody battle between the two forces took place at City Hall. The 7th Regiment was called out by the state, and placed Fernando under arrest.

Through the vicissitudes of the war years, not much more is known about Ida's role in Ben's complicated life than what has already been related. She shared his political convictions, and remained a lifelong Democrat. When he was under attack, she remained loyal; loyalty was one of her dominant characteristics. People no doubt supposed that as a flower of the Old South, born in Louisiana and brought up in New Orleans, she had something to do with Ben's Southern sympathies. With that background, no one would have taken her for an Abolitionist. Yet these are only suppositions, because Ida stayed in the background, except for their social life together, from 1857, when she met Ben, until 1867, when she married him in church.

Meanwhile, it is easy to believe that she took a serious interest in his newspaper, recognizing a good property when she saw one. No doubt she advised Ben about the conduct of his business affairs, for of the two she was much the superior in business judgment.

Ida, one can imagine, had a good deal to do with resuscitating the *Daily News* after the war. Since so much of the city's population had agreed with its stand, it did not suffer severely as a result of the North's victory, and in fact began to prosper as soon as the war was over. During the conflict it had been compelled to raise its price as high as four cents, but as soon as the price of paper came down again, Ben did what the other papers did not do. He brought the price back to one cent, and in 1867 the *Daily News* became the first evening penny paper in the country. It was also on the way to a success it had never enjoyed before, with a five-cent Sunday edition to add to its income. Ten years later it began printing a German-language edition, the *Tages Nachrichten*. There was also in time a weekly edition, whose price Ben succeeded in bringing down from a dollar to fifty cents. All of these extra editions reached high circulation figures.

The highest, however, remained the daily itself. In 1868, Ben proudly added under its nameplate the slogan: "The Largest Circulation of Any Daily Newspaper In The United States," and so it remained for a few years, going from eighty thousand at the end of the war to a hundred thousand in 1870. Yet, paradoxically, it was a newspaper unknown to the city's middle and upper classes. At least among newspapermen, it was jokingly referred to as "the washwoman's gazette." It was read almost exclusively in the tenement-house districts, where both Ben and Fernando Wood's political strength had always been greatest, and to whose prejudices and tastes the *Daily News* had been tailored from the beginning. The news columns were filled exclusively, after the war, with sex, crime, and scandal of the lowest kind; its advertising was on no higher level. Nonetheless it was a gold mine. Ben took out at least $100,000 every year for some time, and some newspaper historians have estimated that the profits eventually ran to $200,000 a year or more.

Ben held his newspaper as a family property, in the customary mysterious Wood way. It had been capitalized in the beginning at only $30,000. Ben owned 80 percent of the stock of the newspaper. The other stockholders were listed as Colonel William Lee Brown, who owned nearly all the remaining shares; George Bartholomew, the managing editor; and "Miss Wood, his sister-in-law," according to his obituary. Who was Miss Wood? As far as the world knew, Ida's only sister was Miss Mary E. Mayfield.

The world, however, knew only a small part of what was going on in Ben Wood's life.

9

BETWEEN THE END of the war and the end of the century, the lives of Ben and Ida Wood took on a further coloration of mystery. There were contradictions and unexplained circumstances, letters which made no sense in the light of the facts when they became known later. They lived, indeed, a life of intrigue at odds with their position as leaders of New York society.

There was, for example, the curious notation Ben made in 1872, when things were not going well for him financially. Found in Ida's effects, this notation declared that properties he supposedly owned on West Eleventh Street and in Williamsburg did not really belong to him, but to Mary E. Mayfield.

To add further to the confusion, the house at 175 West Eleventh Street was purchased, so it was disclosed, in the name of "Mary E. Maifeild," one of the variant spellings of Mayfield found in Ida's notes, but the Williamsburg property was bought by Mary E. Walsh, in September, 1868. It was still in that name when Ben wrote his 1872 notation. Five years later, however, it was transferred from Mary E. Walsh to Mary E. Mayfield, for a consideration of one dollar. Ida was a witness to this puzzling transaction.

Furthermore, when the census reports for these later years of Ben Wood's life were examined, there were strange statements made in them which indicated that the census takers were either haphazard or must have been given erroneous information. In the 1870 census when the Wood family was living at 45 Fifth Avenue, the age of every member was given incorrectly and not all the family was included. Ben was listed as forty-five (he was fifty), Ida was given as forty (she was thirty-two). The children were recorded as Emma, Henry, and Benjamin. Emma and Henry's birthplace was given as Kentucky, Ida's as New York, Benjamin's as Louisiana.

Henry's age was listed as ten. This was inaccurate on two scores. In the first place, there were two Henrys living in the Wood household at the time; one was Ben's son, the other Ida's brother. Secondly, neither was ten years old; both were twenty-one; Ben's son was born June 6, 1849, Ida's brother on December 9, 1849.

By 1880, the family had moved to 175 West Eleventh Street. The head of the house was now listed as Ida's mother. Ben was recorded as a son-in-law, age fifty-nine; Ida as a daughter, age thirty-two (she was forty-two); Emma as a granddaughter, age fourteen; and Henry, a son, age twenty-six (he was thirty-one). This was Ida's brother Henry. Ben's son Henry had in the meantime married, and presumably he lived with his wife at their own residence. Young Benjamin, who was born July 30, 1847, is also missing from the 1880 census of the Wood household. Ben and Ida had agreed that Benjamin, Jr., aged thirty-three when the 1880 census was taken, should be out in the world on his own.

Their birthplaces had changed, too, in the intervening decade. Ida gave hers as New Orleans, Emma's as New York, Elizabeth and Henry's as New Orleans, and Mrs. Mayfield's as simply Louisiana.

Curiously, another resident in the Wood household was recorded in these returns—a girl named Delia Watson. She is first heard of in Manhasset, where she was supposed to be the child of Delia Bowers, or Wood. After that Delia's death, the little Delia apparently came to live with Ben and Ida. In the census of 1870 she appears as a fifteen-year-old child, living with Ben's family, but ten years later she is listed as Delia Watts, aged twenty-seven. In 1860, when she lived in Ben's Long Island home, she was listed as Delia Wood. To further confuse matters, her presumed adoptive mother was listed also in that census as Delia Wood, rather than Bowers.

Who was Delia Watson, or Watts? We were never able to learn. She may well have been a child born of the unexplained relationship between Ben and Delia Bowers. Or she may have been a child of Delia Bowers by some other man, whom Ben undertook to care for.

For Benjamin Wood was not entirely a bad man. He was a sharp businessman but probably no worse than most of his contemporaries in a freebooting, unregulated era. He believed in slavery and secession, and hated Lincoln, but so did hundreds of thousands of his fellow Americans. In the conduct of his newspaper, he appealed to the lowest instincts of his readers, but the front pages of more respectable papers did that every day. And whatever else could be said about Ben, his love for Ida was deep and sincere.

No more touching proof could be offered of his devotion

than the case of Emma, whom he stubbornly presented to the world as his own daughter, because Ida wished it. From time to time it was whispered by his enemies, and even printed, that she was really his adopted daughter. He denied it in public, but it troubled him nonetheless, these anonymous suggestions about Emma's identity. In 1887, after another snide attack, he decided to do something about it. A letter from him found among Ida's effects, undoubtedly given to her by Father Young, who had officiated at Ben's marriage to Ida in St. Paul's Church, revealed an astonishing fact about Emma.

Ben wrote this letter in the course of making a will, in which he was setting up trust funds for his children, including one guaranteeing Emma, "my daughter," $6,000 a year. A doubt rose in his mind as to whether she could be sure of getting it if the will were contested, and so he wrote to Father Young. The following is the full text of Ben's letter, in which he acknowledged that Emma was Ida's sister:

"New York, Oct. 17th, 1887.

"My dear Father Young

"I desire to write you concerning a matter which I wish you to consider as confidential, and not use unless it may be necessary to protect my Daughter Emma in the event of my death. She is as you know only my adopted Daughter but as it was my intention when I took her as an infant to fully adopt her as my own child and to give her all the rights of such a child I have always treated her loved her and educated her as such.

"Wishing her to love me as if I were her own Father I and my wife, whose sister Emma is, have kept the truth from her, and we do not wish her to know it unless it becomes necessary to ward off any attempt that might be made after my death to debar her from receiving in full the legacy I have made to her in my will, naming her there simply as my daughter.

"I have some reason to believe there is some enemy who may attempt to make use of a legal quibble for that purpose as there lately appeared in a Society newspaper a mention of her as my stepdaughter. This I publicly denied over my own signature in several papers for it may have been intended as a slur upon the honour of my beloved Wife, who you can testify has always been a true and faithful Wife to me and who certainly never had any children.

"Will you Father Young please preserve this letter which may be of use to prevent not only the setting aside of my will a thing I do not fear having had it very carefully drawn up, but may hinder even an attempt to do so and thus my beloved child Emma may not be forced to learn the secret I have kept from her solely on account of my own affection for her and to enjoy her affection for myself. Besides I cannot think of any good or happiness to herself to come from telling her now.

"I have given her the place of a beloved child in my heart and home and she has a full right to all I can give her as a child, and I will not rob her of the happiness she has in believing herself to be such, nor deprive myself of the hope of her reverencing and loving my memory as her affectionate Father after my death.

"Yours very truly,
"B. Wood.

"P.S. I wish to inform you that I have left in my will which is in possession of my wife twelve thousand a year income to my wife. To my daughter Emma six thousand dollars a year income. To my sons Benjamin and Henry six thousand dollars a year income and to my sisters Florinda Morton and Albinia Baldwin fifteen hundred dollars a year income, all to have a pro rata income of any amount over the sum provided in my will made from the profits of the properties left by me. I feel positive I will not make another will, and if I should I declare the sum to my daughter shall not be less than the sum named above and never shall be less than the amount to my sons. In my will I left fifteen hundred dollars to my brother Henry Wood but as he is now deceased that sum ceases.

"Yours very truly,
"B. Wood.

"To Rev. Alfred Young
St. Pauls Church
59th Street
New York."

The will to which Ben referred was superseded by later wills which he executed. Indeed, he made eighteen separate wills or codicils during his lifetime. But when he died he left no estate, so his last will was not probated. Consequently there was no occasion on this account for Emma being told that Ida was her sister and not her mother, if that was the case. When the two of them were growing old together in the Herald Square Hotel, was Ida tempted to tell her? Did she tell her? There is no record that she did. Mary must have known, since she was seventeen years old when Emma was born. Did Mary tell Emma, or did she keep Ida's secret? These were among the questions about Ida's life which we were never able to answer, even after the most patient and thorough investigation. All we know is that Emma lived and died, apparently believing she was Ida's daughter.

As Ben and Ida grew old, he continued to indulge her in nearly everything she wanted. If she desired her sister to be their daughter, then his daughter she would be, and he was prepared to fight anyone who said she wasn't. If she wanted her family to live in her home, Ben agreed to that also. Indeed, as we have seen, in the 1880 census Ida's mother was listed as the head of the household.

Ben gave Ida what she had wanted from the beginning—money, jewels, and social position—but he also gave her what she hadn't bargained for: love.

However, Ben was a strong man with strong appetites, and there were certain ways in which he wanted to live his own life. Not all Ida's reproaches could stop him. He gave her soft answers, and did what he wanted to do. She always had the art of hanging on to money; Ben was a talented and careless spender.

His passion was gambling. It was his only diversion. For years he spent nearly all his waking hours playing cards for very high stakes. Once he wagered the *Daily News* itself, and fortunately won. His friends knew him as a *bon vivant,* an authority on food, in which he indulged himself.

Ben often wrote to Ida apologizing for his gambling habits. These letters usually ended, "unfortunately for you, your husband, Ben." But then he would be back next day to John Morrissey's gambling house on lower Broadway, where he won and lost large sums at faro and roulette. On one spectacular night at Morrissey's, he won about $100,000, and driving home in a giddy mood, he woke up Ida and insisted on counting out the money on her bed. At Dick Canfield's famous casino in Saratoga, he was even luckier on another night, winning $150,000.

There were several different stories about how Ida dealt with this passion of her husband's. One was that she often waited outside the club in her carriage to be certain that if he won she would be on hand to get a percentage of his winnings. If he lost, so it was said, she charged him waiting time. If he needed to borrow money to gamble again, she charged him interest.

Another story was that Ida had agreed she would not interfere in any way with his gambling if he would give her half of everything he won and take the losses himself. Three years after this agreement, so the story went, she owned nearly everything he had.

Although he never gave her the slightest reason to doubt his constancy, Ida constantly charged her husband with infidelity. He wrote letter after letter from the Manhattan Club denying it. Finally he wrote one vowing that she was the only woman in his life, and the only one he had ever loved, and declared his willingness to swear to these facts before a competent authority. Following his signature were the words "sworn to me this [date]," a signature, and the words "notary public." Ida noted tidily on the end of this letter, "He offered to swear to this and I had him do so."

There were reports about Ida, too, apparently circulated by Ben's enemies, saying that she had been anything but chaste both before and after her marriage. That was how the story first spread that Emma Wood was the result of an early indiscretion. These rumors prompted the letter already quoted when Ben was making out his will, but it also elicited another a few months later, written from the club on the afternoon of November 24, 1888, which Ben had notarized before he sent it off to Ida.

"I do not attempt to deny that you are a virtuous wife," he wrote, and went on to assert, as he had so often, that he had never had any extramarital affairs of his own. He expressed the greatest confidence in Ida's faithfulness. "Your behavior," he wrote, "has always been above reproach. I do not know how the report you complain of originated.

"You have never lived apart from me. Your whole life, since your fifteenth year, has been in my keeping; and the report that Emma is not my daughter, that she is your daughter and not mine, should not trouble you. There are so many who knew you and me before she was born and know that you were my wife many years before we had a child."

He closed by telling Ida that he had made arrangements to publish in the *Daily News* and in other newspapers a statement to the effect that a report he and Ida were married when she was only fifteen years old was "a malicious lie."

Whatever the explanation for this strange letter—a ruse to distract malicious enemies who might find the letter, or any other—the one element of undoubted truth in it was the faithfulness of both parties. There is not the least reason to believe that Ben and Ida ever strayed from each other after the day they met.

Gambling was Ben's consuming interest, and as a gambler, he had considerable talent. Not only was he daring and knowledgeable, but he had an incredible memory. No one could equal him as a ready reckoner or a master of mental arithmetic, disciplines which aided him greatly at the green table.

An inveterate follower of politics, whether in or out of office, he combined his experience and his memory in frequent displays of election predicting. He boasted, and often proved it, that on election day, if he were given the results from a few districts, or scattered data from any state, he could predict the result.

Ben was not a heavy drinker, but he was a formidable smoker, consuming half a box of cigars in a day, although he smoked barely half of each one. In 1885, for some unexplained reason, he gave up smoking entirely.

He apparently lost some of his proficiency at the gambling table as he grew older. He began to lose so heavily that in 1897 creditors who had lent him large sums of money threatened to petition him into bankruptcy. He was compelled to find some means of obtaining a large loan. There was only one person in the world he knew with a lot of money whom he could trust, and that was Ida. She had managed to save a fortune in spite of his extravagances, and so he turned to her. It was a business deal. Ida gave him the money, and in return he sold her his controlling shares in the paper. A year later, accompanied by Ida, Mary, and Emma, he was off to Europe and Egypt for a trip which occupied nearly another year before they came home in December, 1899. He was ailing with rheumatism. He was still editor-in-chief of the *Daily News,* and although he had never gone back to the office after he borrowed the money from Ida, he continued to read galley proofs and page proofs at home, which was then a suite in the old Fifth Avenue Hotel, on Madison Square.

Ben was reading proofs until three days before his death, on the day before Washington's birthday, 1900. The obituaries were kind to him. Some of them scarcely mentioned his Civil War activities. The *Times* noted that "it was said yesterday that Mr. Wood possessed no real estate and that his personal property was of small value." It was true, in a sense. Nearly everything he owned was in Ida's name by this time.

As a woman who was accustomed to having her own way, Ida imagined that she could operate the *Daily News* as well as anyone. Nothing could have been further from the truth. She had no knowledge of newspaper management, and made no particular effort to get along with Colonel William Lee Brown, Ben's second-in-command and a minority stockholder.

Ida was interested at first only in the business side of the paper, but she soon discovered how completely interconnected it was with the editorial side, and it was not long before she was sitting in the editor's chair. As an editor, Ida was unusual, even in a city which had produced some notable eccentrics. She began to make sweeping changes as soon as she took over the paper. Her first act was to cut down on the reporting staff, and when the editors protested, she explained that if news were worth publishing it would flow automatically into the office, consequently fewer reporters would be needed.

There was also too much "tampering" with the news, Ida declared. News was better in its original, pristine form, she said. By the time it dawned on the editors that she was taking a stand against editing, several of them had been fired.

While the editorial department was shredded, the composing room basked in Ida's managerial smile. She had a high regard for printers because, as she truly said, the paper could not be put out without them. She was equally approving of the subscription and advertising salesmen because they brought in the money. She promised them all raises, but the increases were never forthcoming.

It was Ida's belief that there was no reason for an editor of a newspaper to be on the premises, and so she did her editing from her suite in the Fifth Avenue Hotel, keeping a corps of copyboys busy shuttling back and forth with stories, editorials, and advertising copy. She checked, blue-penciled and censored everything that was published. Occasionally she wrote an editorial, always supporting whatever the Democratic Party might be advocating. She ordered the editors who remained to emphasize human interest stories, and oddly enough, she was particularly interested in any story which had to do with recluses. Could her ultimate plan already have been in the back of her mind?

As editor, Ida abandoned most of Ben's precepts and methods, but she did retain his policy of keeping the paper's price at a penny. On her explicit instructions, the newsboys roamed the street crying: "*Daily News,* one cent—Help mother pay the rent," which must have seemed a sharp contrast to the slogan the new owner of *The New York Times* was proclaiming, "All the news that's fit to print."

Under the best of circumstances the *Daily News* might not have survived in a city where William Randolph Hearst's *Journal* and Joseph Pulitzer's *World,* after their epic circulation battle during the Spanish-American War, had very nearly saturated the same market the *Daily News* was trying to reach. But under Ida's mismanagement, it had no chance at all. In little more than a year she alienated the entire staff, and ruined a once valuable newspaper property. It was ripe for sale to Frank Munsey, known as the Grand High Executioner of journalism, who was making a career out of buying and merging newspapers, and thus reducing the number of papers in New York.

Munsey bought the *Daily News* from Ida in 1901 for $340,000. Characteristically she insisted that he pay her in thousand-dollar bills, and Munsey, amused by this idea, agreed. He made up the money into packages and sent them to her by one of his bright young men, William T. Dewart, who later became president of the New York *Sun*. There was a bizarre little ceremony in Ida's parlor at the hotel, in which Dewart, at Ida's insistence, counted out every dollar of the money before her eyes. Then Ida counted it herself, and put it away before she turned over to him the keys of the *Daily News*.

Purchasing the paper proved to be one of Munsey's major mistakes in a career during which he was right often enough to amass forty million dollars. He nudged Colonel Brown out of his minority holdings, and proceeded to "improve" the paper, which turned out to be the one thing guaranteed to put it out of business entirely. The clientele of the *Daily News* did not want an improved paper. They wanted the familiar one, with all the dismal pre-Ida faults they had known and loved for years. Readers and advertisers alike began to leave the new and better *Daily News* until in 1904 a thoroughly disgusted Munsey virtually gave the paper to one of its employees for a nominal figure. It was too late for rehabilitation, and the paper died two years later. Munsey was reported to have lost $750,000 in his misguided effort to reform Ben Wood's paper.

Left without Ben, but in possession of enough money to do anything she liked, Ida spent several years in traveling with Mary and Emma. They traveled throughout the United States, then went on cruises to the Mediterranean and jaunts about Europe.

As she grew older, Ida's dread of dying in poverty gripped her in a strangling fear. One day, as she was walking along

Fifth Avenue, she met one of her friends, a banker. As they talked, he told her he was concerned about the country's financial situation (it was the onset of the Panic of 1907), and particularly about the difficulty some banks seemed to be encountering.

It was all Ida needed to hear, in her growing state of financial anxiety. Ida recalled the Panic of 1873, when major New York banks failed during a five-year depression which ensued. Bank failures were also characteristic of the four-year-long depression which followed the Panic of 1893. She asked her friend for advice, and he told her it might be a good idea if she withdrew her funds from the banks, and placed them in a safe-deposit box until the financial crisis was over. As we have seen, she lost no time in doing it.

She apparently put her funds in a safe-deposit box which she shared at the time with Mary and Emma. Our investigation yielded records which showed that the three had a box at the Safe Deposit Company of New York from May 1, 1881, to the year 1913, when they surrendered it and leased a box at the Lincoln Safe Deposit Company at 1187–1201 Third Avenue in Manhattan. They maintained this box until April 10, 1928. The safe-deposit company's records showed that during the 1913–1928 period the box was opened a dozen times, always by Mary.

Ida lived at the Fifth Avenue Hotel with Ben when he died in 1900. She continued to maintain her residence there while she owned the *Daily News*. Afterwards, during her travels with Emma and Mary, her Fifth Avenue Hotel residence was little more than a mailing address. The years of travel were perhaps symptomatic of Ida's growing lack of interest in her New York surroundings.

Slowly there developed in her a desire for obscurity. With Mary and Emma, she moved to the Herald Square Hotel in late 1907, where they registered as residents of Philadelphia. The records of the Lincoln Safe Deposit Company showed her residence as "Continental Hotel, Philadelphia, Pennsylvania." Mary paid their rent for the box at the Lincoln Safe Deposit Company in the course of personal visits, obviating the need for mailing rent bills.

At the Herald Square Hotel, Ida, joined by Mary and Emma, slowly withdrew from the world into the twilight domain of the recluse, where death found first poor Emma in 1928, then Miss Mary in 1931, and at last the strong-willed Ida herself on March 12, 1932.

10

WITH IDA'S DEATH, the real drama began.

Otis Wood's role as the committee in charge of Ida had come to an end, except for giving an accounting of his stewardship, as required by law. On March 17, 1932, the O'Brien firm, as his attorneys, offered for probate the will Ida had made on July 9, 1889. The will was written in Ida's hand. Her signature, "Ida E. Wood," was witnessed by Ben, who signed "B. Wood," and by one R. F. McCormack. Each of the witnesses also signed as subscribing witnesses, Ben giving his address as the Fifth Avenue Hotel, McCormack as 233 East Thirty-second Street. The legal language of the will indicated that Ida either copied in her own hand a draft prepared for her by a lawyer, or adapted to her own use a form of will written by a lawyer for someone else. The text of the will was as follows:

"IN THE NAME OF GOD, AMEN, I, Ida E. Wood Wife of Benjamin Wood being of sound and disposing mind and memory, and considering the uncertainty of this life, do make, publish and declare, this to be my last WILL and TESTAMENT, as follows: First, after my lawful debts are paid, I give and bequeath to my Sister Mary E. W. Mayfield, And to my Daughter Emma Wood, both of them now residing with me at the Fifth Ave Hotel New York to the above named Emma Wood And the above named Mary

Elizabeth W. Mayfield I give devise and bequeath all my property real and personal and mixed of what nature and kind so ever and wheresoever the same shall be at the time of my death To be divided share and share alike between them for their own use forever to use or dispose of as they may wish if either die before me the one who survives shall take and keep for herself the whole of my property real and personal whatever I own at the time of my death.

"I hereby appoint my sister Mary Elizabeth Mayfield Sole executrix to be Executrix of this my last Will and Testament: hereby revoking all former Wills by me made I will that the said Mary E. Mayfield shall not be required to give Bonds or security of any kind for the faithfull execution of the duties of executrix.

"IN WITNESS WHEREOF, I have hereunto subscribed my name, and affixed my seal, the Ninth day of July in the year of our Lord, one thousand eight hundred and Eighty Nine."

The two Wood factions were still at odds. When Otis filed his application for probate of Ida's will, the other faction, led by Mrs. Shields, petitioned the Court to have one of their group appointed temporary administrator of Ida's estate. On April 23, 1932, over the protest of Otis, Surrogate Foley granted temporary letters of administration to Ben's great-grandson Henry Wood, jointly with the Bankers Trust Company. This was a victory for the Shields faction.

The victory was inevitable. The Shields faction consisted of the grandchildren and the great-grandchildren of Ben by his first wife, Catherine Davidson, who had died before Ben married Ida. Though not blood relatives of Ida, they were Ben's direct descendants, and as such they were nearer in relationship to Ida than nieces or nephews who were collateral relatives, including nephew Otis Wood.

Emma and Mary, the only beneficiaries under Ida's will, had predeceased Ida without leaving any issue. This would not, of itself, preclude probating of the will. It would be necessary, however, to prove its valid execution.

One of the subscribing witnesses to Ida's will, her husband Ben, had predeceased Ida. So far as the other subscribing witness, R. F. McCormack, was concerned, no one could find out who he was or whether he ever existed. That the subscribing witnesses are dead or are absent from the state does not necessarily preclude the Surrogate from admitting a will to probate. Proof of the handwriting of the subscribing witnesses may be taken without their personal testimony under certain circumstances to substantiate the proper execution of the will.

Ben's signature could be proved, but no proof was available of the handwriting of the unidentified "R. F. McCormack." Accordingly, on August 22, 1934, Surrogate Foley denied probate to Ida's will. While denying probate to the will, however, the Surrogate held that, "The signature of the testatrix [that is, Ida] has been established as authentic." This judicial finding which identified Ida's handwriting would play a significant part in the case. The Surrogate also held that the handwriting of the subscribing witness, Benjamin Wood, "has likewise been proven."

In his decision which denied probate to the offered will, Surrogate Foley took account of the situation as it then existed. More than two hundred claimants, he noted, had asserted varying degrees of kinship to Ida. In view of the rejection of Ida's will, there was no reason for the temporary administrators—the representatives of the Shields faction—to continue their functions, since their appointment was for an interim period pending the outcome of the proceedings for the probate of Ida's will. Concluding, Surrogate Foley directed the Public Administrator to apply for letters of administration on Ida's estate.

The Surrogate also undoubtedly took heed of the fact that neither of the feuding factions would be interested in finding blood relatives of Ida, since this would eliminate the members of both factions from sharing in the estate.

Acting upon the Surrogate's direction, the Public Administrator applied for letters of administration, which were granted August 30, 1934. It was now my job as Counsel to the Public Administrator to find out who Ida E. Wood really was.

The Public Administrator is an appointed official. There is one in each of the five counties of New York City and in several of the more populous counties of the state. He administers the estates of persons who die leaving neither a valid will nor any relatives who can readily prove that there is nobody more closely related to the decedent and who are willing to administer the estate. He is often required to ascertain the identity or whereabouts of heirs or next of kin entitled to share in the estate.

Many of the estates administered by the Public Administrator are quite small. In these cases he arranges for the burial of the decedent in the city cemetery. Some estates, however, are substantial. In those instances he arranges for burial, assembles the assets of the estate, and pays all taxes and proper debts.

It is the duty of the Public Administrator to take possession of all the belongings of the deceased, including papers and documents which might shed light on his relatives. In addition, all possible information bearing upon the dead person's background is obtained from neighbors, places of employment, banks, hospitals where he may have been a patient, and the Police Department.

When the Public Administrator's efforts to ascertain the identity or whereabouts of heirs or next of kin prove fruitless, he gives public notice of the settlement of the estate by the Surrogate. The balance of the estate after payment of its obligations is thereafter turned over to the city treasury, and five years later to the State. During this period, or at any time thereafter, persons proving a right to the estate or any part of it are entitled to payment.

In Ida's case I followed, at least at the outset, the normal investigative procedures which were incidental to my duties as Counsel to the Public Administrator. I did not perceive immediately the formidable legal and investigative responsibilities which the case would entail. Some investigative work had been done in connection with the proceedings which resulted in the finding that Ida was legally incompetent. That investigation was incidentally directed toward establishing Ida's closest kin, a task difficult in itself because, as she had said in her troubled last years: "My relatives didn't have any use for me. I've lost track of them." My job was different; I had to prove who Ida was, and identify her parents.

At the outset I examined the voluminous records in Ida's incompetency proceeding, in an endeavor to obtain clues as to who she might really be. The Surrogate turned over to our office more than five hundred letters the court had received from people claiming to be related to Ida. Each letter was read and a card index system was established, setting forth the name and the claimed relationship. After the appointment of the Public Administrator became public knowledge, many more letters were received, and each was similarly examined and catalogued.

All the papers found in Ida's rooms in the Herald Square Hotel were taken into custody by Otis Wood after his appointment to safeguard Ida's property and affairs when she was declared an incompetent. Otis delivered them to the Bankers Trust Company, which was appointed one of the temporary administrators of Ida's affairs when her 1889 will was offered for probate. Bankers Trust, in turn, delivered them to the Public Administrator after his appointment as administrator of Ida's estate.

My associates and I went through every one of these papers (many of them in Ida's handwriting, others written by Ben), making notations of anything that might be relevant, and this information too was catalogued. The papers and other written notations which littered Ida's rooms at the Herald Square Hotel were read over and over again, as well as the writings found in the trunks at the Manhattan Storage Warehouse, and the records compiled by the nurses of what Ida had said to them in the last year of her life.

Everywhere we looked, as we examined these records and other clues, contradictions appeared, along with tantalizing views of Ida's real past hidden away in her mysterious notations.

For example, the records showed clearly enough that Ben Wood had married Ida in 1867. Emma's death certificate contained a statement as to her date of birth which would make her ten years old at the time. Yet here was Ida in her 1889 will referring to Emma as her daughter. Various papers and other writings in Ben's hand which came into our possession recorded Ben's repeated insistence that Emma was his and Ida's daughter.

In carrying on my investigation, I went to the Paulist Church, and examined the original record of the 1867 marriage of Ida and Ben. I noticed there was a notation in the book that it was a mixed marriage, and that dispensation had to be obtained. Communicating with the Chancery Office in New York, I got a copy of a letter Father Young had sent to that office, which read: "Dear Father Preston: Please record the dispensation used by me for Benjamin Wood and Ida Ellen Walsh as *mixtae religionis*. Married on the 25th October." The marriage register in the church had been signed: "Ida Ellen Walsh Mayfield." This was a startling disclosure. Why did Father Young's letter omit the "Mayfield?" How did the name Walsh fit into the picture of Ida's background?

Other puzzling documents picked up in Ida's rooms linked her to that name. One was an undertaker's receipt given to a Mr. Thomas Walsh for the burial of his son in September, 1846, in a cemetery in Cambridge, Massachusetts. Another was a similar receipt, given to Mother Russell, of the Sisters of Mercy in San Francisco, for the burial of a Thomas Walsh in Mount Calvary Cemetery there, in November, 1864.

Bits of paper found among Ida's effects challenged our ingenuity. They were odd pieces of information which seemed to be saying something—old papers speaking from the past in cracked and faded voices—but what they said could not be heard at once.

Two sheets of paper, both in Ida's handwriting, commanded my attention. I would not realize for some time how important they were in unraveling the mystery of Ida's identity. The writing on each sheet seemed similar in content, but there were differences. The first sheet, a blank piece of paper, read as follows:

"May 17th, 1881
"This paper is a copy taken from an old memorandum.
"E. Sunday between 2 & 3 pm–Jan 14/1838
Old
La
"M. Monday afternoon May 11/1840
Lee
York

"M. Friday night betwen 12 & 2 December 7/1850
Salem

"L. Tuesday Noon April 7/1852
Cambridge
"E. Wednesday Morning between 2 & 3 Feb 10/1857
Ma"

The second sheet of paper was stationery from the Caux Palace Hotel at Territeh-Montreux, Switzerland. At the top of the sheet was a picture of the hotel. Ida wrote as follows:

"This paper is a copy from old memorandum.
"E. Sunday between 2 & 3 pm Jan 14th 1838 O
"M—Monday afternoon May 11th 1840 Lee
"M J—Friday night between 12 & 2 o'clock Dec. 7th 1850—S
"L Tuesday noon April 7th 1852 C
"E Wednesday morning between 2 & 3 o'clock Feb 10th, 1857 M"

The statements made on each sheet were essentially the same. The writing on the Switzerland hotel stationery omitted the date set forth on the top of the blank sheet, used "O" in place of "Old La," "Lee" instead of "Lee York," "S" for "Salem," "C" for "Cambridge," "M" for "Ma," and

"M J" for "M." Otherwise the message in each was identical.

But what was this message on the two sheets, which I called the "Old Memoranda" in my discussions of them? Each sheet stated it was a "copy" of an "old memorandum," but we were unable to find any other memorandum, old or otherwise. Perhaps Ida destroyed it because it was too revealing. Perhaps it never existed.

We had no way of knowing whether both sheets were written at the same time. We sensed they contained important information, else Ida would not have written the information separately on two sheets, and preserved it so many years.

We had a feeling that if we could decipher the hieroglyphics of the Old Memoranda, it might help to unravel the mystery of Ida's identity. There seemed sufficient basis for speculating that these memoranda could be a record relating to Ida's family. Could it be, we pondered, that the initials at the beginning of the first two lines were those of Emma and Mary? Their ages, however, did not coincide, and we were left at sea by the absence of any initial for Ida.

Who was L? Possibly another brother, Louis, whom she had mentioned in her rambling reminiscences to the nurses—"the wild one," as she called him. A lady in Pennsylvania thought differently, however, when she read about the Old Memoranda after they had been reported in the newspapers. "L," she wrote, must be her Aunt Lorinda, who had a sister Ida married to a Benjamin Wood.

"Old La" might mean Louisiana, but no locality could be found in that large and fertile state to explain the word or the abbreviation "Old." The burgeoning Mayfield claimants, however, were considerably heartened by the notation, especially those letter writers who traced their relationship to three Mayfields who had emigrated from Ireland early in the eighteenth century and settled in South Carolina. A Mayfield lady wrote that a very old woman in that state had told her she had seen Ida and Mary Mayfield when they had visited the old Mayfield Manor.

There might be, we thought, a correlation between the word "Cambridge" in one of the sheets of the Old Memoranda, and the receipt given to Thomas Walsh for the burial of his child in a cemetery in Cambridge, Massachusetts. So we sent an investigator to Cambridge. The cemetery custodian verified that the location indicated on the receipt did, indeed, refer to a portion of the cemetery. But when the site was examined, it was found to be covered by tufts of grass and earth. Our investigator gave us the discouraging report that no gravestone was visible.

I read again some of the conversations the nurses had remembered, and here was Ida saying: "My mother was married to Mr. Mayfield, and Mary and I were their children. But my father went with other women—oh, he was a rascal! —and so my mother divorced him. When I had money of my own, I gave him enough to go out to California, and he died out there."

That cast some light on the reason Ida had kept for almost seventy years the receipt given to Mother Russell for the burial of a Thomas Walsh in San Francisco. I concluded this lead should be followed up at once.

An examination of hospital records in San Francisco showed that a man named Thomas Walsh had, indeed, died there in 1864. His birthplace was given as County "Mead" (obviously meant to be Meath) in Ireland. Mother Russell, who had borne the expense of burial and had been given a receipt for it, proved to be a sister of Sir Charles Russell, later the Lord Chief Justice of England, Baron Russell of Killowen, of a County Down family. Three of her sisters became Sisters of Mercy, and Mother Russell herself had gone to California as early as 1854, in response to the desperate need there for nursing sisters. For years she had maintained an active correspondence with one of her sisters in Ireland, which was made available to us, but an examination of it failed to disclose anything at all about Thomas Walsh, or why it was that Mother Russell had borne the expenses of his burial.

We sent an investigator into the hinterlands of South Carolina, where he examined the vital statistics of the citizens of Leeds and York, two villages near the Mayfield Manor, on the supposition that "Lee York" in the Old Memoranda referred to these villages. But if Miss Mary Mayfield had been born in either of these places, the records did not show it.

Nor had she or any other Mayfield been born in either Salem or Cambridge, Massachusetts, we learned, after we had painstakingly worked our way through the records in those communities.

While these investigations proceeded, I was all but overwhelmed by an ever-increasing number of letters, mounting into the hundreds, from various places in Louisiana, written by persons who asserted they were relatives of Ida. I therefore requested my able and energetic associate, Joseph T. Arenson—who later succeeded me as Counsel to the Public Administrator when I was elected a Justice of the New York State Supreme Court—to go down to Louisiana in an effort to find out all he could about those persons who were claiming relationship to Ida, and to see if he could uncover evidence bearing upon the possibility that Ida might really be a Louisiana Mayfield.

While Arenson was engaged in his Louisiana search, I had a telephone call one morning from the Corporation Counsel of New York City, who told me he had been informed that a will of Ida's had been discovered in Louisiana.

News of this will came as a bombshell to all of us. It brought our investigation to a halt. If the will were genuine, no need would exist to learn the true identity of Ida or to discover her heirs, since her estate would be distributed in accordance with the terms of that instrument, by the person entitled to administer the estate under the will.

All my attention, consequently, was directed now toward this new document, which might effectively end the search for Ida Wood when it was no more than begun.

11

I SENT A TELEGRAM to Arenson immediately, instructing him to go to a small town in Louisiana, about sixty miles from where he was at the time, and to interview there an attorney whose name had been given to me by the Corporation Counsel. This lawyer, who had once been the district attorney in a small Louisiana town, was alleged to have the will in his possession.

Arenson found his man in one of those dusty Southern villages that breathe age and inertia. His office was a drab frame house, entered by two steps from the street level. There was no waiting room; as soon as Arenson opened the door he found himself in a disorderly little room, unfurnished except for a desk and a chair or two. Behind the desk sat the lawyer, a thin, almost scrawny man who rose to a lanky six feet as his visitor entered. His red suspenders held up loose-fitting khaki trousers, and he was chewing tobacco. He certainly did not look the part, but a large sign out in front had proclaimed LAWYER in block letters. Arenson noted professionally, however, that there were few law books in the office.

By this time it was five o'clock in the afternoon, and the lawyer, after the preliminaries were over, announced that it was too late to show Arenson the will that day. These preliminaries had consumed about forty minutes, and were unusual in themselves. Arenson first had to convince the lawyer that he really represented the Public Administrator, after which, rolling his tobacco wad, the Southerner put his visitor through an inquisition, asking questions about the estate, how many people from the South were claimants, and similar inquiries. Arenson told him only facts he believed were matters of public record, meanwhile noting that his inquisitor did not appear to be familiar with the law of wills and estates.

At length the lawyer, seeing that Arenson's patience was tried, hesitatingly answered a few questions. The will, he said, had been found in a Bible in a trunk, and he had had it in his possession only a short time. He had known the legatee mentioned in the will for a long period.

"The will is in a safety-deposit box," he told Arenson, ending the interview. "I'll meet you tomorrow morning at ten o'clock at the bank, and we'll examine it together. Then I'll send it to the Surrogate's Court, as you suggest."

But when Arenson arrived next morning at the appointed hour, the lawyer did not appear. After waiting an hour or so, Arenson called the attorney's home, and discovered he had slipped off to New Orleans. As it turned out, he had gone to the bank earlier that morning, removed the will from the box, and taken it to New Orleans to have it photostated, after which he mailed the original will to the Corporation Counsel in New York City.

Arenson was confirming some of these facts independently. He had driven the sixty miles to New Orleans at once, and by making the rounds of the few photostating services in that city, had discovered easily what the lawyer had done. On a chance, he telephoned the elusive attorney at his office and found him in. He had changed his mind, said the lawyer, and decided to send the will to the New York City Corporation Counsel, rather than to the Surrogate's Court.

While he was in New Orleans, Arenson learned that the lawyers in that city had been discussing the Ida Wood story for some time, following it in the wire service stories and especially in a recounting of the case in the Hearst Sunday supplement, *The American Weekly,* which was widely read in the South. The New Orleans papers had also reported that a representative of the Public Administrator (Arenson) was in New Orleans, interviewing Mayfield claimants.

The Corporation Counsel's office viewed the new document with particular interest when it was received and read. The will's terms provided that the City of New York would get half of Ida's fortune. With this possibility in mind, if the document proved genuine, the office immediately sent an assistant to New Orleans.

When we had an opportunity to examine the will after it was filed in court by the Corporation Counsel, we thought it an odd document indeed. Written in pencil, it read:

"New York Sept. 15th, 1896. this is my Second and last Will I Ida Mayfield Welch Wood in case of Mary and Emma Death I request and want one half of my cash and Jewelry given to truader Carpenter at my death she is the daughter of John Quincy Carpenter who was good friend of mine when I was in trouble in my young days also a cousin to my Comon law Husbin thomas Welch after thomas Welchs death I Married Benjamini Wood I leave the other half of my Cash and Jewelry to Ney York City My——[illegible] forsaken by my family when I was a young girl and I know nothing of them."

Beside the names of the witnesses, Hardy Carpenter and Dean Givens, a postscript had been added: "I am Writing this in the back of my old bible for you to give to truader Carpenter at my death." The will was signed "Ida Mayfield Welch Wood."

If one were to accept this as Ida's will, he would have to believe that she was an illiterate person. True, she was occasionally careless about spelling and punctuation, as some of her letters showed, but it was impossible to believe she could ever have written a document reflecting such illiteracy. As owner of the *Daily News,* she had acted as its editor. From histories of journalism we had learned that she composed editorials and wrote them in her own hand. She even corrected the language of editorials written by seasoned newspapermen to suit her own ideas of expression, unprofessional though these ideas were.

We thought that the will was a forgery for this reason alone. Then we compared its writing with the authenticated sample of Ida's handwriting on file in the Surrogate's Court. It will be recalled that Surrogate Foley, while denying probate to Ida's 1889 will, had held that her signature to the will "has been established as authentic."

A comparison of Ida's authenticated signature with the handwriting of the Louisiana document satisfied us that they were not written by the same person. Feeling confident that the document would be rejected by the court, we felt free to go ahead with our investigation of Ida's identity while the invalidity of the Louisiana document was being established. We already had sufficient evidence of discrepancies about Ida's past to indicate that much time-consuming as well as arduous work needed to be done to establish her true identity.

Whoever was behind the Louisiana will had been clever indeed. "Truader Carpenter" proved to be Mrs. Truda Carpenter Hammond, of Ponchatoula, Louisiana. The will had been produced by one of her descendants, who was not contending that the money had been left to him, but to his mother, Mrs. Hammond, who had survived Ida and then died without leaving a will of her own. The legacy to Mrs. Hammond would therefore go to her estate under New York law, and her next of kin would in turn inherit from the estate.

The fact that the will was written in pencil was another ingenious touch. Handwriting experts cannot tell the age of a writing in pencil, as they can with one in ink. It is much easier to forge in pencil than in ink because the pencil marks rub and become hazy in the course of time, while ink, though fading, remains exactly as written.

Then, too, if the will were declared a forgery, no one could be prosecuted criminally. The crime, if any, would be attributable to the deceased Mrs. Hammond, who was a beneficiary under the will. Her son, who had found the will after her death, could claim that he was doing no more than what he was required to do by law in producing it. Her son, we ascertained, did not perpetrate the forgery and, so far as we were able to learn, he did not participate in it.

Perhaps the most artful touch, however, was the bequest to the City of New York, thus ensuring that the claimant would get free representation from the largest law firm in the world, the city's Corporation Counsel.

We did not wait for the will to be offered for probate by the Corporation Counsel. Instead we immediately petitioned for a denial of probate and set about to prove that it was a forgery. We employed an expert in paper, parchment, and similar materials who told us after a careful examination that he was able to recognize the watermark on the paper, showing that it had not been manufactured until several years after the 1896 date of the will.

The Corporation Counsel's office called upon Francis D. Murphy, of the Police Department's forgery squad, to act as its handwriting expert. He made a searching comparison of the writing in the will with Ida's known writings. As a result of this study he could do no more than demonstrate that certain similarities existed between the writing on the Louisiana will and Ida's authentic handwriting.

Elbridge W. Stein, the expert we had engaged to prove the will a forgery, was a specialist with long experience in questioned documents. His opinion bore considerable weight. Stein's testimony helped to convince the court that Ida was not the person who wrote the Louisiana will.

Surrogate Foley was sharp in his denial of probate to this second will. "The instrument," he declared bluntly, "is clearly a forgery." Whereupon he granted the application which I had made as counsel to the Public Administrator to deny probate.

Now that the forged Louisiana will was out of the way, I could turn my time and attention once more to the search for Ida Wood's identity.

12

As I WENT THROUGH the bits of paper, notations and letters Ida had left behind, it often seemed to me as though I were trying to fit together the pieces of a jigsaw puzzle, but it was not too long before some of the material began to take on meaning.

One of the most valuable documents we found in Ida's belongings was what came to be called "the rose-colored notebook." Like the Old Memoranda, it was in Ida's handwriting. It was undated, and bore the stamp of a New Orleans stationery firm. I came to call that notebook the Rosetta Stone of the Ida E. Wood mystery.

The rose-colored notebook told the story of the death of Ida's mother, and in telling it provided valuable clues to Ida's identity. "Mother," Ida wrote, "died one p.m. midday July 6, 1883 Aitkins Hotel Room No. 16 114 Argyle St. Glasgow Scotland. Buried in Del Beth Cemetery Glasgow Tuesday July 10th."

"Mother's remains," Ida continued, "were removed from Scotland to New York, placed in the receiving vault at Calvary until the monument was finished in Nov 1884 then placed in our plot Section 9, plot 41 on the 15th of Nov. 1884."

Ida had saved much material about her mother, which

confirmed the circumstances of her death, her burial and her reburial, as described in the rose-colored notebook. There were newspaper accounts of her mother's death, and a Glasgow death certificate showing that her maiden name was Crawford and that she was the widow of "Henry Mayfield, sugar planter." The same statement appeared in Rode's *New York Directory* for 1872, which listed a "Mary E. Mayfield, widow of Henry."

Ida's mother had come to live near Ida, first in the house in Williamsburg, perhaps with Miss Mary, later with the entire Wood family in the Eleventh Street house. In 1883 she expressed a desire to see her relatives and prepared to make the trip—but not to Louisiana, supposed home of the Mayfields. She sailed for Scotland. Unfortunately, before she could see anyone, she suffered a heart attack, and died shortly after arriving there.

As soon as Ida learned, by cable, of her mother's death, she and Ben left for Scotland. Arriving there, Ida behaved in the determined fashion that characterized her life. Cutting her way through Scottish red tape, she had the body exhumed and brought back to New York.

It was impossible to trace the steps by which this was accomplished. Neither the authorities in London nor those in Edinburgh could account for how Ida managed to get her mother's body taken from the grave and out of Scotland. By this time, however, it appeared that Ida could do anything.

While it was kept temporarily in a vault at Calvary Cemetery in New York, Ida bought a large plot and prepared to have a handsome monument erected on it. This was to be no hasty reinterment. Ida meant to create an enduring memorial. A faded note in her handwriting showed that she prepared the first inscription herself. No sooner was the bill from the mason received, however, than Ida's brother Henry died. Ida insisted on having the monument redone to include him. She asked the mason to give her an estimate for "taking down the monument, erasing it, re-polishing and re-setting the monument." Ida wrote as follows about Henry's death in the rose-colored notebook: "Henry died Jan. 3rd, 1885 Saturday half past 9 p.m. Room 233 5th Ave Hotel New York, Buried in Calvary Cemetery Jan. 7th 1885. On the 7th of Jan. 1885 my brother Henry was buried beside our mother."

It was in the rose-colored notebook that we also found a notation which bore an obvious relation to the receipt for the burial of Thomas Walsh in San Francisco, found in Ida's room. The entry read: "Father arrived in California August 6th, 1862. Died Nov. 9th at 10 a.m., 1864. Buried November 10th in Mount Calvary Cemetery, California."

This was an important clue indeed. The entry confirmed the burial receipt, and both appeared to indicate that Ida's father was really a man named Thomas Walsh. But over in Calvary Cemetery in New York City, the family history Ida had caused to be engraved on the monument stated, equally plainly, that Thomas Henry Mayfield was her father. Could it be that Ida had both a father and a stepfather? That was one of the numerous mysteries which had to be solved.

If Ida had both a father and a stepfather, could she have gotten the order of her mother's husbands reversed? Supposing she had been married to a Mr. Walsh, who died in San Francisco, could she have later married a Henry or a Thomas Henry Mayfield? In that case, however, Ida could not be a Mayfield, born and bred. Thomas Henry Mayfield was not mentioned in the rose-colored notebook.

More family history was unearthed in the material which was being examined. I found correspondence about Ida's brother, Henry Benjamin Mayfield, who died in 1885. Ben, apparently, was fond of Henry, and treated him like a son. When he had to go to Cincinnati on business having to do with the Louisiana lottery in which he and Fernando were profitably involved, he took Henry with him. There was evidence, too, that when Henry grew up and became a lawyer, he had some kind of affiliation with the celebrated law firm of Howe & Hummel. Bill Howe and Abe Hummel had written notes to Henry expressing their regard for him, and Ida had saved them. There were also a few books from the Howe & Hummel library which Henry had borrowed or had been given.

Ida had a low opinion of lawyers, and apparently it was based partly on Henry's inability to earn much money out of his practice. "Young lawyers don't get much pay," she was fond of saying. Henry got so little that he was dependent on his sisters all his life. It may have been because he was never strong, and could not stand up under the long hours an important case might require. Ida was willing to help him, but at the same time she couldn't conceal her irritation that Henry had not gone into something more lucrative. He must have been a likable man, however, and not without friends in high places, because a good many of the political notables of the time were mourners at his funeral.

Oddly, there were few references in the old letters and documents to Miss Mary, but what little there was seemed complimentary. Ida evidently thought well of her sister because Mary was, in Ida's words, "a good business woman." Ben was helpful to Mary in her business transactions. In her name, he negotiated various real estate and other deals, including the purchase of the house on Eleventh Street.

From the letters a portrait of Mary slowly emerged as an extremely helpful and dependable person. Her actions were in complete harmony with Ida's ambitions, and she submerged her personality to Ida's dominating will. When it was time for Emma to be sent to school in France, it was Mary who took her, and when their mother made her last pilgrimage to Scotland, it was Mary who accompanied her. While subordinating herself to Ida, she somehow never lost her sense of proportion or her sense of the fitness of things. In the faded photos which were taken from the trunks, her pleasant, rather pretty face gazed out calmly with an air of poise and distinction.

Miss Mary died as she had lived, unobtrusively. Ida supplied for the benefit of her death record the information that she was born in the United States, and that her father had been Thomas W. Mayfield and her mother Mary A. Crawford, both "born in Ireland."

An examination of the trunks also revealed a great deal of information concerning Emma's tragic life. While the most startling disclosure had already emerged, that she appeared to be Ida's sister, the death record found among Ida's stored-up documents showed that she had died at seventy-one, meaning that her birth must have been in 1857. Consequently, when Ben and Ida were married in 1867 in the Paulist Church, she would have been ten years old. The marriage, and everything it implied for Ida's ambitions, was so important to her that immediately afterward she took pains, with her husband's help, to make the world believe that Emma had been her child by Ben, born after the marriage.

When the Federal census takers came around in 1870, it will be recalled, Ida listed Emma as her daughter and gave her age as fourteen, which was exactly right. But that was only because it would have been impossible to pass her off as a child of four. In the census of 1880, however, when the Woods and Mayfields were ensconced in the house on Eleventh Street, she was again listed as fourteen, although by that time she was twenty-four. Poor Emma stayed fourteen for ten years.

She was sent to school at the Ursuline Convent in New Orleans, where Ida intimated vaguely that she had spent her young Mayfield girlhood. My associate, Joseph Arenson, searched the records of the convent for the period when Emma was a student. The pages relating to Emma, he learned, had been torn out of the book, by whom or for what reason we were never able to learn. But it appears that after two years in the convent school, Emma spent a year in a New York academy before Mary whisked her off to France to finishing school.

While most debutantes in New York were emerging at the usual eighteen, Ida for some reason postponed Emma's coming out until 1892, when according to the official reckoning she would have been twenty-five. She was, of course, thirty-five, but she looked young; in a sense Emma never really grew up, completely overshadowed and dominated as she was by Ida. Like her brother Henry, whom she believed to be her uncle, Emma was not strong. Ida took her frequently to doctors. One of her troubles was diagnosed as double curvature of the spine. Emma was a hunchback who never grew to full stature, although her deformity was well disguised. This undoubtedly aided Ida in her pretense that Emma was twenty-five when in fact she was ten years older.

Emma's debut took place at Delmonico's, the most fashionable restaurant in New York, and in a style that befitted Ben Wood's position in the city. More than two hundred people attended. A pathetic note to Ben's granddaughter, Mrs. Blanche Wood Shields, conveyed poor Emma's elation about this first and only high point in her life. "No married people except Mamma and two other ladies as Chaprones," she wrote excitedly, displaying her mother-sister's carelessness with spelling. "We will have a splendid supper, the ball room will be decorated with Flowers I expect to have a lovely time."

One hopes she did. There were to be few other lovely times in her life. Dutifully smiling, she simply faded into the background of Ida's career, never marrying.

The debut was only one of many deceptions practiced in her behalf. During the year before, she had been admitted to membership in the Daughters of the American Revolution. In the record submitted to the society by her supposed father, Ben, through whom she was eligible, her birthplace was given as New York for the first time. It had always been New Orleans before. The D.A.R. ladies hesitated a bit after the documents were submitted. After all, although Ben's ancestors had certainly fought in the Revolution, his own conduct during the Civil War could hardly have been considered patriotic. Perhaps, too, they had heard the recurring stories circulated about Emma's not being Ben's real daughter. In any case, there were delays, but Ben's influence, spurred by Ida's insistence, succeeded at last in getting the application approved.

Poor Emma complained—at least once as a matter of record, and probably much more often—that there were no young men in her life. When she made this sad confession in a letter to Ben, he wrote back that he would see to it that the situation was corrected. Somehow, and it would be fascinating to know how, he kept his word. It was not long afterward before Emma announced her engagement. Then, inexplicably, she broke it. After that there were no men in Emma's life at all, except Ben, who faithfully assured her in every letter he wrote of his deep paternal affection.

Of all the clues the trunks and notebooks and documents yielded up, one of the most important was at the outset the most obscure. That was the letter written to Ida in 1866, when she was living in the house on West Fifty-fourth Street as Mrs. Benjamin Wood, a year before her church marriage. This letter, written by the Superior of the House of the Angel Guardian, in Jamaica Plain, Massachusetts, thanked Ida for a gift and acknowledged receipt of ten dollars "for Michael."

We followed up this clue immediately. A letter to the Mother Superior at the Massachusetts school, asking for information about a "Michael" registered as Mayfield, or possibly Walsh or Welch, brought a quick reply. Yes, wrote the Mother Superior, there had been such a boy admitted on March 29, 1866, a Michael Walsh, aged fourteen, born in Salem, Massachusetts. His father was listed as Thomas Walsh, deceased; his mother as Ann, living. Under the heading "person responsible," the school form carried the necessary linking information: Mrs. Benjamin Wood, of 213 West Fifty-fourth Street, New York.

If Ida had a brother named Michael Walsh, as seemed probable, could this Michael be the Henry Mayfield who grew up to be a lawyer? But what about the other brother, Louis, the "wild" one who was "drowned up in Massachusetts," the one Ida had talked about in her rambling conversations with the nurses? There must surely have been two brothers.

I re-examined the rose-colored notebook: "Louis died May 21st, buried May 23rd, 1865." The receipt for the grave in the Cambridge Cemetery, on the other hand, had been dated 1846. Louis, then, could not be Ida's brother whom Thomas Walsh had buried in Cambridge in September 1846, according to the burial receipt which had been found in Ida's room.

A search of the New York papers of the period failed to yield any record of Louis's demise. Then we tried the files of the Boston newspapers, and in one of them, the *Daily Evening Traveler* for May 22, 1865, this obscure paragraph was found: "Drowned. A boy named Welsh, about twelve years of age, was drowned in a creek, rear of the rubber factory, at Malden, yesterday afternoon. His parents reside in Edgeworth." With this information to guide us, it was no task to find in the State House in Boston, among the vital statistics, official confirmation of the *Traveler's* story: "Welch. May 21, 1865, Louis, 13 years. Born in Cambridge. Parents, Thomas and Ann Crawford Welch." In spite of the variant spellings, it seemed fair to conclude that this unfortunate boy was Ida's brother, Louis Walsh.

Returning now to the Old Memoranda, we concluded that

"L. Tuesday afternoon, April 7, 1852," followed by "Cambridge" in one of the sheets and by "C" in the other, referred not to Louis's death but to his date of birth. Louis was born in Cambridge, Massachusetts, on April 7, 1852, and died by drowning in Cambridge on May 21, 1865.

I found it increasingly difficult to believe that nothing remained of the burial place of the dead brother mentioned in the 1846 burial receipt given to Thomas Walsh. If Cambridge was the burial place of that brother, it would normally be the burial place of Louis as well. Perhaps others might be buried in a family plot. This speculation was bolstered by the discovery in Ida's effects of a receipt for the payment for a monument in the Cambridge cemetery. If we could find it, it might be the key which could unlock a good many other mysteries. I determined to go to Massachusetts myself, and make another search.

13

THE CATHOLIC CEMETERY in Cambridge, Massachusetts, is a small piece of New England, crowded in now by metropolitan Boston. I had asked the caretaker to bring a shovel with him, because I was convinced there must be some further proof of Ida's identity lying in that place where at least one Walsh child had been buried. Louis, I believed, was also buried there. I meant to find the headstone if it were there. The 1846 receipt specified that a boy had been buried in Lot G. 14 R.I. East.

Families kept their burial receipts in those days as title deeds, to be used when there were later burials in the same family. Eighty-five years after the 1846 receipt was issued, it had turned up in Ida Wood's room in the Herald Square Hotel after her death. It was this document which led me to Cambridge on a bright September day, when a soft wind from the Charles River sent the brilliant autumn leaves fluttering over the headstones.

Deep grass, seared half brown by the summer sun, lay in a tangled mass over the lot. Draping his jacket on a nearby gravestone, the caretaker began probing and digging with his shovel. "Seems to be indented here," he observed after a time, between grunts, and applied his shovel to the place.

In the still air of the cemetery we could hear the bite of the shovel as it plunged again and again into the turf, and then the sharp, metallic "ping" as it struck against something beneath the surface.

That sound of metal on stone was the key turning in the lock which had barred us from Ida's past. With more digging and some hoisting on our part, we unearthed a headstone. It was easy to see what had happened. Long ago it had toppled from its pediment, lain neglected, and earth and grass had covered it where it lay, face downward.

We turned it up to the mellow September sun, and carefully scraped away the dirt and clinging grass until it stood clean and revealing before us.

The inscription read:

"Erected by Ann Walsh in memory of her husband Thomas Walsh who died in Sanfrancisco Nov. 8, 1864, aged 54 years.

"Thomas Walsh, died September 11, 1846, aged 11 months.

"Also an infant son, died 1847.

"Margret Walsh, died August 28, 1859, aged 60 years.

"Louis N. Walsh, died May 21, 1865, aged 13 years."

Thomas Walsh was the man Ida had referred to in her rose-colored notebook as "father." It also seemed clear that the Ann Walsh who had put up the stone must be Ida's mother. If not, how could it possibly be explained that the Ann Crawford Welch who was Louis's mother was someone different from the Ann Mary Crawford, mother of Ida and Henry, who was named on the New York monument?

The stone further confirmed that Louis, the drowned boy, whose death had caused the monument to be erected, was indeed Ida's brother. He was the "L" in the Old Memoranda, born April 7, 1852, in Cambridge, and according to the account of his death in the Boston *Traveler,* his parents were living at the time in Edgeworth, a part of Malden.

All this seemed to confirm that Ida must have been a Walsh, and we remembered that she had signed her marriage register as Ida Ellen Walsh Mayfield. She had been married in a Catholic church to a non-Catholic, requiring a dispensation. It was the one place where a woman would certainly be asked about her baptism and the name given to her then. As a priest, discharging his duties properly, Father Young had to be sure about the baptism of the Catholic party to the marriage. When he made out his report for the Chancellor, he left out the name "Mayfield."

The stone in the Cambridge Cemetery also put to rest the mystery of the undertaker's receipt given to Thomas Walsh for the burial of his son in September, 1846. The receipt related to the infant Thomas. Ida had kept this receipt close to her in her rooms at the Herald Square Hotel.

Now we turned to the "Margret" Walsh on the stone. Comparing the date of her death with that of Ida's father, Thomas Walsh, indicated that "Margret" could very well be Thomas's mother, Ida's paternal grandmother. This assumption seemed to be confirmed by what we found out shortly thereafter from people living in Malden. We sought out anyone who would have been likely to know the Walsh family, and incredible as it might seem, there were old friends and neighbors still living who remembered them.

One of them was Mrs. Margaret O'Reilly, who was a little flustered by her visitors but asked them to sit down, settled back in her rocker, and told them her story.

Certainly she had known the Walshes. She was eighty-two years old, was Margaret O'Reilly, and her memory was clear for events long past. She had been Margaret Griffin then, six years old in 1857, having been born on the safe waters of Massachusetts Bay in 1851, just before her parents, immigrants from County Kerry in Ireland, landed in the New World.

The Griffins lived on Oakland Street in Malden. Down the road a little way lived the Walshes and their children. By coincidence, Margaret Griffin's mother had also been a Walsh, and for this and other reasons the two families quickly became friends. One of the other reasons was the shop Mr. Walsh's mother kept in a front room of the house, where Margaret Griffin spent her pennies for candy and cookies. This modest storekeeper, it seemed to us, was the "Margret" Walsh of the tombstone in the Cambridge cemetery.

Margaret Griffin O'Reilly was full of memories. Rocking away and answering questions, flattered by all the attention she was getting, she searched the past, and nearly everything she said produced more facts relating to Ida Wood's real identity.

"I remember there was a baby in the family named Emma," she said. "And there was Mary Ann, and Louis, and yes, there was another brother named Michael. My, I remember the day Louis was drowned. We all remembered that, it was so terrible, the way he just wandered off down behind the old rubber plant, and next thing we knew someone came running and said, 'Louis is drowned.' I'll never forget it.

"I remember a young woman used to come up from New York and visit the Walshes, a very pretty young woman. She had the most beautiful dark eyes I ever saw, and long dark hair. All the Walshes called her Ellen, but when they talked about her to us and the other neighbors, she was always 'Mrs. Harvey.' Whenever the lady from New York came for a visit, the word would go around the neighborhood—you know how people talk—and everybody would whisper, 'that lady is at the Walshes' house.' And when she left, they'd whisper all over again, 'The lady at the Walshes' house has gone back to New York.'

"I used to like to go to the Walshes after the new baby was born. Mrs. Walsh would let me watch her bathe and dress little Emma. There was something wrong with that child, I noticed right away—something wrong with the poor little thing's back. Every time her mother dressed her, it seemed to hurt her back, and she would cry, and sometimes Mrs. Walsh would cry too, and that would make me feel so bad I'd join right in. But I'll never forget the day Emma was all dressed up in her best Sunday clothes, and her mother took her off down to New York. 'We're going to visit Mrs. Harvey,' she told everyone. They came back in a week or two, and Emma was dressed up in clothes even better than the ones she'd gone away in. They were the most beautiful clothes I ever saw."

Later we looked back in the dusty files at Malden, recording births and deaths, and there we found that "Emma Welch" was born there February 10, 1857, that her father was Thomas and her mother Ann.

It appeared, then, that Emma was the "E" of the Old Memoranda, with the notation following, "Wednesday morning between 2 & 3 o'clock, Feb. 10th, 1857." The cryptic reference to a place, "M" on one memorandum and "Ma" on the other, meant Malden. This, we had reason to believe, was the same Emma whom Benjamin Wood had taken into his home ten years later and passed off as his and Ida's child.

We continued to probe Mrs. O'Reilly's memory. We wanted to know if she could throw any light on another line in the Old Memoranda, the one that read, "M., Friday night between 12 & 2 o'clock Dec. 7, 1850 S." In one memorandum the place was "S," in the other it was written out as "Salem." We asked Mrs. O'Reilly what she could tell us about Michael, the other boy in the Walsh family she had recalled. There her memory failed her. We had to look elsewhere for Michael, and we found him in the register of the Church of the Immaculate Conception, in Salem, Massachusetts. There was recorded the baptism of an infant named Michael, child of Thomas Welsh and Mary [*sic*] his wife, on December 16, 1849. According to the register, the child was one week old on that date. In the notation in Ida's Old Memoranda the date recorded was December 7, 1850.

These were puzzling discrepancies. Although the month in the register was the same, there was still the matter of a year's difference in the dates, and the fact that the mother's name was given as Mary, not Ann.

The fascinating thing about this discovery, however, was that it led to the linking of Ida's brother, "Henry Mayfield," with Michael Walsh. They were apparently different names for the same person. Michael's school record showed that his age was the same as that of "Henry," and the birthplace of both was given as Salem. He was listed as Michael in the Malden census of 1855 as five years old, living with his mother and father, Thomas and Ann, his sister Mary Ann, his brother "Lewis," and his paternal grandmother Margaret. Ida was not listed. Five years later, only Ida's father Thomas and his grandmother Margaret were listed in the Federal census for Malden, but that was because Ida's mother Ann Walsh and Emma were in New York visiting "Mrs. Harvey," as Ida was then known, and having their pictures taken. By 1865, the Malden census recorded the sad fact that "Ann Welch" was living as a widow at forty-five, with only "Lewis," ten, and Emma, seven, to keep her company. Five days after this entry was made, Louis was drowned, at the age of thirteen. Age discrepancy was then common in census taking.

The spelling discrepancies, also, were easily explained. Census takers, and in fact all keepers of public records, wrote by ear in those days, and errors were common. That accounted for the spelling of "Walsh" as both "Welsh" and "Welch." On Thomas's application for letters of administration on his mother's estate, when she died, his name appeared as "Welsh, alias Walsh."

Before taking leave of Mrs. O'Reilly, we touched on a subject which Ida had spoken about to the nurses. In one of her outbursts over being deprived of her liberty, Ida had cried out: "The only boss I've ever had in this world was my father. My husband and my mother always let me have my own way. If my cousin in San Francisco only knew about the trouble I'm in, he'd come and get me out." His name, she had added later, was Terence Fitzpatrick. However, an inquiry which I had caused to be made in San Francisco had produced no one by that name.

Mrs. O'Reilly remembered him. "Oh, yes, Terence," she said. "He was Grandmother Walsh's favorite. His father was Matthew Fitzpatrick, a young fellow from Ireland. He worked down at the brickyard in Cambridge for a while, and then he got into real estate. Matthew married a sister of Thomas Walsh, and when she died Terence went off to sea in a whaler. I think that was about 1858." Presumably Terence's journey ended in San Francisco.

We now decided to locate, if possible, the home where Ida's family, including her paternal grandmother Margaret Walsh, lived in Malden. Luckily, we found the old Walsh home still intact on Oakland Street. The front room where Ida's paternal grandmother, Grandmother Walsh, sold her candy and cookies was unchanged. Leafing through the registers of real estate transactions kept in the Malden courthouse building, we determined that Grandmother Walsh had been its owner, and we were able to follow her progress from 1848 to 1859.

Malden was a growing village in those days, and Ida's Uncle Matthew Fitzpatrick bought a lot and built a house on it, with a brick foundation. He sold it to Grandmother Margaret Walsh, the records showed, and she lived in it from 1848 to 1853. It was not far from the cemetery in which she would one day rest.

Matthew bought some more land in 1853, near the Medford boundary, and built a double house there, selling seven rooms in it to his sister-in-law, Grandmother Walsh. That was where the Walshes were living when the census of 1855 was taken.

By this time, Uncle Matthew had real estate fever. When the Edgeworth subdivision was opened, he built a third house, which Grandmother Walsh liked so well that she sold back the seven rooms to him and bought the new place in

January, 1857. In this house, according to the records, poor Emma was born the following month. Grandmother Walsh established her little shop there, and neighbor Margaret Griffin came to visit. Two days before she died in 1859, Grandmother Walsh deeded the house to her son Thomas, Ida's father, and in June, 1862, on the eve of his departure for California, he sold it to his daughter Mary, Ida's sister. Two months later Thomas, according to the rose-colored notebook found in Ida's possession, was in California.

It was Louis's death in 1865 that finally ended the Walsh era in Malden. Less than a month after he was drowned, Ida's sister Mary sold the house, and with her brother Michael, her sister Emma, and her mother, came to New York to live, and there the Walshes were transformed, in a manner and for reasons we did not yet understand, into Mayfields.

By 1872, Ida's mother Ann Walsh, widow of Thomas, a hawker or itinerant trader, had become Mary E. Mayfield, widow of Henry, New Orleans sugar planter; her daughter Mary had become Mary E. Mayfield, and her son Michael had become Henry Mayfield.

Miss Mary contributed to the confusing name changes by her own real estate transactions in New York. The Eleventh Street House, it will be recalled, was bought under the name of "Mary E. Maifeild," but the Williamsburg property was purchased under the name of Mary E. Walsh, in September 1868. When the curious transaction of 1877 occurred, and Mary E. Walsh conveyed the Williamsburg property to herself as Mary E. Mayfield for one dollar—was that an effort to obliterate any further record of the Walsh name she brought to New York?

Just before she sailed for Glasgow with her mother, Mary

sold the Williamsburg property. It was one of the few business deals in which she took a loss—it had cost her $5,000 and she was compelled to sell it for $4,000.

The Williamsburg property, we concluded, was probably the house where Ida's mother lived between 1865 and 1872, after which all other trace of her is lost. Presumably, when the family moved from Malden to New York, Mary bought the house for them to live in until Ida could do better for the family—although the money for the house must have flowed from Ben to Ida to Mary.

Our investigation turned up a photograph, apparently one of Emma, taken by a Williamsburg photographer between 1867 and 1870. We found, too, that the last photograph known to have been taken of Ida's mother was the work of another Brooklyn photographer named Biffar.

This photograph was enlarged, colored, and a good artist had painted the portrait of Ida's mother from it, undoubtedly at Ida's instigation. She emerged as a *grande dame,* and that too was what Ida wanted, because she looked as though she might well have been the widow of a rich Louisiana sugar planter named Mayfield. Ida loved the portrait. She had a photograph taken of it, and kept it with her until the day she died, along with other portraits of herself, Mary, and Emma, all as young women.

Thus the Old Memoranda, the rose-colored notebook, the undertaker's receipt given to Thomas Walsh for the burial of his son in 1846, and the record of Louis's drowning had led us to Cambridge and had given us documentary support for our growing belief that Ida Wood was not a Mayfield but a Walsh, and, according to the record, she must have been born Ellen Walsh, the name which appeared in the middle of her marriage registry signature in the Paulist Church.

The evidence which we had accumulated seemed to point to the transformation from Walsh to Mayfield. We still did not know why the change was made, but we plunged into the investigation with renewed hope. We thought we were getting closer to the real facts about Ida's identity, and when we had those, we might be able to explain the great deception which had been her life.

14

MY INVESTIGATION up to this point appeared to establish the identity of Ida's paternal grandmother, Margaret Walsh; her father, Thomas Walsh; and her mother, Ann Crawford Walsh. We knew, too, that all these people, as well as Ida's known brothers and sisters, were dead. What we did not know was the history of the Walshes before 1846, when Ida's little brother Thomas was buried in Cambridge. We still did not know where Ida was born, or where her sister Mary was born, or where Ida lived before she came to New York. To establish these facts, and thereby further to clarify Ida's identity, we concluded it would be necessary to delve deeper, and determine the ancestors and families of Thomas Walsh and Ann Crawford.

Some of these avenues were being explored while we were still completing our investigation in Cambridge and Malden, but in the search for these still unknown ancestors of Ida's, she had unfortunately left us no little rose-colored notebook or Old Memoranda, full of valuable clues, to guide us.

What she did leave, however, were rambling statements she volunteered to her nurses, which they recorded and passed on to the investigators. Some of these notes were incoherent, some were inconsistent with others, but after we re-examined them, they sent us off in a new direction.

"My father was Irish and my mother Scotch," she declared on one occasion. "Her father was well known in Dublin, and everybody knew him as a good man."

On another night, she had remarked to a nurse: "I remember my old aunt, my mother's sister Mary. She had a baker's shop in Dublin."

There were other fragmentary pieces in Ida's conversation about Patrick Crawford, her mother's father, who was a Dublin baker, a man who was good to the poor, and gave them every day the "crumpled loaves," as the villagers called them, meaning the stale bread he couldn't sell. She talked, too, about a pair of Crawford cousins of whom she was fond. They were children of her "Uncle Patrick," she said, who had been left in the care of her "Aunt Eliza, in Salem."

That turned us toward Salem again. The Salem records were searched to find a trace of Patrick Crawford. There was such a man, a baker aged forty-three, who had died on January 14, 1857, but there the trail ended. Whether it was the same Patrick Crawford or another, I could not determine.

In this impasse, a break in the case not brought about by us opened up the lead we needed. The O'Brien firm, it will be recalled, had acted as attorneys for Otis Wood in offering for probate Ida's 1889 handwritten will in which she had left half her property to Emma, the other half to Mary. Probate was eventually denied.

While the application for probate was under consideration, however, Ben's great-grandson Henry Wood jointly with the Bankers Trust Company were granted temporary letters of administration over the objection of Otis. The O'Brien firm then indicated they would like to withdraw as attorneys for Otis. At the suggestion of Surrogate Foley, however, they remained in the case while the probate proceedings were pending. The Surrogate took the view that the law firm had a duty to seek the persons who were Ida's next of kin, and apprise them of their rights.

In the office of the O'Brien firm was an employee, not a lawyer himself, named J. C. Walsh, a former newspaperman who had edited papers in Montreal and Toronto. Intrigued by the mystery of Ida's identity, Walsh decided on a newspaperman's shortcut in attempting to solve it. In the course of his work he had become acquainted with a clerical employee of the Boston *Globe,* Elizabeth McNaught, who had been a client of the firm in a matter before the Surrogate's Court. Walsh conceived the notion of running an ad in the Boston *Globe* and a feature story in connection with it about Ida's case. He wrote the article himself and gave it to Miss McNaught, permitting her to have it printed under her byline if she could persuade the *Globe*'s publisher to allow publication of the ad and the story. His hope was that among the paper's readers there might be some who would read the article and remember the Crawfords.

The publisher hesitated at first. There was the obvious risk that still more people wholly unrelated to Ida, attracted by cupidity rather than kinship, would be added to the rising list of claimants to her fortune. It could be depended upon that some of these would be poor people, in danger of being victimized through their unfounded expectations. But eventually he decided to take the risk in view of the fact that it was an exciting story.

The piece was given prominent display in the Sunday edition; the advertisement running in the same edition employed the Biffar photograph of Ida's mother, taken about 1870. The story itself carried a picture of Ida and two of her mother. The reasoning was that copies of the 1870 picture, particularly, might well have been sent to relatives at the time.

Walsh's article was cleverly constructed, giving no hint that it might be useful to anyone except those who could identify the Walsh family out of their own knowledge. The bold headlines surrounding the picture of Ann Walsh were in the paper's characteristic style: BOSTON RELATIVES OF WOMAN WHO HID MONEY IN HER SKIRT. New York Lawyers Trying To Pierce The Veil of Century—Mrs. Ida Wood Died With Fortune in Hotel Room With Her—Wanted Money To Go To Uncle's Children, Who Work in The Revere House.

The last statement must have sprung from J. C. Walsh's active imagination. In the story, the whole quotation read: "See that my property goes to my uncle's children; you'll find them; they work in the Revere House and live somewhere in Boston." And the reporter added, "That was the whisper to anyone in whom she thought she could confide."

If Ida ever confided this wish to anyone, in a whisper or not, it had never appeared elsewhere. Walsh apparently inserted it in the story simply to inspire a response. But the article did disclose to the Boston public for the first time that the Walshes were involved in the Wood case. All the previous stories had favored Mayfields and Crawfords.

Since the pictures that appeared with the story were the most important part of the *Globe* article, it is worth noting the meticulous research we had already undertaken to identify and catalogue these daguerreotypes found in Ida's trunks. Sometimes the boxes they were kept in bore the name and address of the photographer, and by consulting city directories over a period of a few years, it was possible to find out whether a particular photographer had been at the address given during a two- to five-year period. Since the ages of the Walsh children had been established by the census returns, it was no great task to identify the pictures.

In the systematic manner of her earlier days, Ida made an effort to sort out the pictures, and put them in some kind of order. She had a good many photographs of herself, from youth to middle age, and in all of them she appeared as the slim, dark beauty she truly was, with eyes whose extraordinary brilliance conquered even the old prints. There was a set of pictures of her mother, taken in the later daguerreotype period, at a time when the printing of copies from a negative had not yet come into vogue. Anyone who wanted more than one picture had to sit for each additional shot. In that case the custom of photographers was to alter slightly the position of head and hands. One of these pictures of Ida's mother, Ann Walsh, was reproduced in the *Globe* article, along with one of Ida at the height of her beauty.

The response was what one might have expected: a deluge of letters from Walshes and Crawfords everywhere in New England. Nearly all of them were quite obviously of no value. Then came a letter from a lady in Salem named Katherine J. Sheehan, which fulfilled Walsh's expectations. Mrs. Sheehan wrote:

"In answer to request in Boston Globe . . . for pictures of Ann Crawford wife of Thomas Walsh, present my claim, having picture identical with the earlier one as my grandmother named

Eliza Crawford O'Connor is her sister. She married Thomas O'Connor and came to this country with my mother Eliza Jane and two other children, namely: Mary Ann and Winifred, and lived at Lowell, Newburyport, Peabody, and then settled in Salem, Mass., living at 9 Prince St. There were six more children born in this country namely; Emmaline, James, Thomas Francis, Michael, and two Catherines. My grandmother lived many years with my mother and as a child I heard many stories from her about the bakery in Dublin, and her sister Ann and children Ellen and Mary. Approximately about 1891 Mary Walsh, daughter of Ann, visited relatives here and asked for pictures of the family to take with her. Grandmother died a few years afterward and was buried from my home."

The letter went on to list the only living relatives "as far as I know."

A lawyer from the O'Brien firm went up to see Mrs. Sheehan immediately, taking with him photostats of the daguerreotypes of Ida's mother, Ann Walsh, for purposes of comparison with the one she possessed. When they were compared, there was no doubt. Ann Walsh was the lady in both pictures.

The lawyer had also brought along a rather large tintype of two elderly women. If one of these women was Ann Walsh, as he believed, the other might be her sister, Eliza Crawford O'Connor.

"Do you know either one of these women?" he asked Mrs. Sheehan.

Before he had the words out of his mouth, Mrs. Sheehan exclaimed, "There's Grandma!" and pointed to the photograph of one of the women.

Here then, at last, was the Aunt Eliza whom Ida had

spoken of, who had taken care of Ida's two Crawford cousins, the children of her Uncle Patrick.

At the end of the interview with Mrs. Sheehan, the lawyer leaned back and considered. He found himself surrounded by Aunt Eliza's grandchildren, pleasant and unpretentious people. He liked them, and wished he could reassure them about their inheritance, but after all, they had nothing more than a photograph of their grandmother. This did not establish with reasonable certainty that Ida's mother Ann and Eliza Crawford O'Connor were sisters.

Aunt Eliza could have made it all clear, of course, but she had died nearly forty years before, and for almost fifty years before her death she had lived entirely in New England, most of the time in Salem. All that her descendants knew about her before she came to America was what they remembered of her talks with them and with their parents. That, however, was not inconsiderable. Like most old women, she had loved to talk about her youth, and especially about the bakery in Dublin where she had spent her girlhood.

That bakery was a strong link in the chain. Ann Walsh had spoken about it to Ida frequently, just as Aunt Eliza had talked about it to her children and grandchildren. In Eliza Crawford O'Connor's family, the bakery was a living tradition whose memory she kept green with reminiscence on every possible occasion.

Ida, of course, had never said anything about the bakery as long as she was a member of New York society. It would hardly have fitted in with the background of one who was, according to the newspaper accounts of her wedding to Ben, "a descendant of the Earls of Crawford." But when she was virtually imprisoned by the nurses in that last year of her life, her mind disjointed by old age and illness, recalling the past in fragments, she talked about the baker and the "crumpled loaves" he gave to the poor. Eliza told the same story, but in her version the expression was "the cold bread."

Eliza's favorite story about her Dublin girlhood, and one she told over and over, concerned the bread riots, when angry, hungry people marched down the streets, breaking the windows of the food merchants. One day a mob came down the street and stopped in front of the bakery where Aunt Eliza lived with her father, Patrick Crawford. They would have broken the windows and taken the bread, Eliza said, but the leader commanded: "This man has been good to the poor. Move on!" Both Ida and her aunt Eliza were fond of the baker who was so good to the poor.

But now, I felt, we were dealing with family legend and hearsay. The search for Ida Wood's real identity as Ellen Walsh, which we would need to prove later on in court, inevitably led to Ireland, and to England as well because it was there that many of the events described by Mrs. Sheehan took place, and supporting documents, if any, would be found. I soon found myself following Ida's trail across the ocean, back to her origins in the British Isles. There lay the beginnings of the mystery, and the clue to some of Ida's motivations.

15

I HAD NOT SEEN IRELAND for nearly twenty years, and as I walked the gray stones of Dublin again, I could not help remembering the days at the end of the first World War when I had seen it last.

At that time I was a member of the 107th United States Infantry, a part of the 27th Division, under command of Major John F. O'Ryan. Both the 27th and the 30th Divisions of the United States Army were brigaded with the British Forces under the command of General Douglas Haig. After the armistice was signed, I was given a furlough, and visited London, Edinburgh, Belfast, and Dublin.

In Dublin another kind of war was going on—the Black and Tan Uprising—and I found myself in the midst of it, wearing my odd combination of American and British uniforms; we had run out of American uniforms. Now, almost two decades later, here I was in Ireland again.

I had arrived with only a few meager clues pointing the way toward Ida's Irish family connections. One was an unidentified photograph taken in Dublin, which we had found among Ida's effects in an old trunk. On its back was a faded inscription; only the word "Dublin" was decipherable. Another clue was embodied in two slips of paper and an envelope in Ida's handwriting. These items bore several Dublin addresses: "Mrs. Margaret Larkin, 42 Summer Hill; Mary Kennedy, 148 Upper Abbey Street; P. Kennedy, 128 Great Britain Street."

There were also the stories both Aunt Eliza and Ida had told about the baker Patrick Crawford in Dublin, and the bread riot in which his bakery was spared from destruction because it was known that he had been kind to the poor. Finally, I had the knowledge derived from Ida's statements and the records in Malden that Ida's parents, Thomas and Ann Crawford Walsh, were born in Ireland.

I began my investigation by working to establish the existence of Patrick Crawford as a Dublin baker. At once a formidable obstacle presented itself. When I went to the great records center, the Four Courts, where birth, death, and marriage certificates are kept, I discovered that most of the documents for the years we needed had been destroyed during the civil war of 1922, when the Record Office, attached to the Four Courts, stood in the path of the rebellion, and was burned. Not only were the census figures lost, but the registers of most of the Church of Ireland parishes were incinerated as well.

Not all these church records were in Dublin, however. The centralization had taken place about 1870, after the Church was disestablished and the people no longer had to pay tithes for support of churches they did not attend. A good many of these churches combined their record keeping, and in such cases there was a danger that the registers of the individual churches might be lost. To prevent these losses, the government directed that all existing registers be sent to Dublin for safekeeping.

Loud protest arose from some of the churches over this action, and the government had to effect a compromise measure. If a church had a safe or vault where the register could be kept, an exception would be made, and the registers would not have to be forwarded to Dublin. In some cases, although the churches sent their registers to Dublin, they had copies made before doing so.

As it turned out, almost all the registers in the counties which were essential to our inquiry had been sent to Dublin, and had been consumed in the fire. Fortunately, records existed of the registers that had been retained by the various churches. In a volume titled *The Twenty-eighth Report of the Deputy Keeper of the Public Records,* published in May, 1896, the records that had been sent to Dublin for safekeeping were printed in heavy type while those that still remained in the possession of the various churches were printed in light type. From an examination of this report we were confronted with the fact that about 60 percent of the possible sources of information concerning the Crawford family had been sent to Dublin, supposedly for safekeeping, and had been destroyed by fire.

We applied to the churches which had kept their records, and although our requests were treated with exceptional courtesy, the results were extremely disappointing. Even where records were available, they were lacking in essential information. Many of the baptismal certificates contained only the Christian names of the parents and rarely, if ever, was the mother's maiden name given. The marriage certificates we examined seldom listed the names of the parents of the couple being married.

Wherever they existed, the registers of the Catholic

churches in both Ireland and England were more informative, but in a great many churches there were no records kept at all. For example, from 1790, the year in which Ida's paternal grandmother Margaret Walsh was born (according to the information contained in her death certificate; we were unable to find her birth or baptismal certificate) until well into the next century, much of Ireland was in a turmoil, and records were not kept in the Catholic churches.

In those troubled days, when a priest built his church at the risk of his liberty and possibly his life, the baptism or marriage was more important than the record of it. Most Catholic infants were baptized at home. Even when the Catholic churches were permitted to resume their activities, the custom persisted. Some Dublin churches kept a separate register later for those baptisms performed at the home of the parents.

For a generation after the repressions of 1798, Catholic places of worship in Dublin were known as "mass houses," and they were tucked away on obscure streets. The church locations were often known only to the people who attended them. After the terror was over, the old customs would not die. It remained customary when referring to a church to say "Meath Street," or "Francis Street," rather than to designate the church by the name of its patron saint, its proper name. The Pro-Cathedral itself was commonly referred to as "Marlboro Street."

As a result of all this confusion, our first efforts to establish the existence of Patrick Crawford, baker, ended in failure. We turned next to the family legend of the bread riots which Aunt Eliza and Ida had passed down. In searching through the Annual Registers, I found that the Annual Register for

1826 noted that there had been several bread riots during the year. Checking these incidents against the newspapers, we found this report in a Dublin newspaper of September 7, describing a court proceeding:

"Between seven and eight o'clock yesterday morning a number of men assembled in James Street and proceeding to the house of Mr. Dempsey, a baker, where they demanded bread, which was given to them; they then went on to the shop of Mr. Manders, where they made a similar demand, which was complied with. The party next proceeded in the direction of Bow Bridge, and on their way, in Irvine Street, they met a boy in the employment of *Mr. Crawford, a baker,* going out with a basket of bread, which they secured and divided among them. On the appearance of a party of police from the Array Quay division, the mob dispersed without committing further outrage."

This story I regarded as a significant find, for while it did not confirm the family legend, it did verify the existence of a baker named Crawford. We examined a map of Dublin and looked into the records concerning all the streets involved in the incident described. Among the deeds filed in King's Inn, I found an 1820 lease by Mary Crawford of a property in Bow Lane. The records also showed that a Patrick Robert Crawford had been buried from 53 Bow Lane on June 16, 1827, and that the Crawford family still lived there in 1830. From the Bow Lane address, we learned, a Michael Kennedy had married Mary Crawford in February, 1829.

But we were blocked from confirming through the census records that a Crawford family had lived in Bow Lane, because those records had been destroyed in 1922. We looked in the mercantile directory of Dublin, but it recorded no bakery in Bow Lane before 1834, and no Crawford bakery anywhere in Dublin at any time.

In the directory of 1834, however, there was a bakery at 53 Bow Lane, where the Crawford bakery was supposed to be, and although the proprietor was listed as James Ward, it could be inferred that the Crawford bakery had been on the same site. We interviewed several old-time residents of the neighborhood with reputed long memories, and several of them told us they had heard that a "small back house" behind Number 53 had been used as an oven in times past. We found it still there.

Further investigation in the musty records of Dublin produced a faded document which proved that there were Crawfords at No. 53 Bow Lane in 1830. That was the year King George IV ordered what was called a "Valuation" of Dublin, with the findings to be published by Parliament, which was done in 1833.

A "Valuation" was a device to help churches collect tithes, the system by which a tenth of a person's produce from the land, or its equivalent in money, was contributed to the regular support of the church. Authorized by various statutes, city ordinances, or customary local practices, depending upon the particular time or locality, the Valuation was an estimate or appraisal of an individual's property or income. Collecting tithes was not a problem in the country, because the churches were well acquainted with the few houses and their occupants within a parish. The Dublin Valuation listed every house in the city, and the amount of "minister's money" due from each occupant was specified. The same list could be used by the grand jury, which was then in charge of the city government, whenever it was necessary to levy a "cess"—a tax—to raise money for public works. The cess was figured in multiples of the "minister's money," and it was a charge on the parish.

Looking into the part of the Valuation applying to the Parish of St. James, where Bow Lane was located, we discovered this highly pertinent information: "House number for the parish, 369. Number in street, 53. Owner or occupier, Crawford. Annual value, 7 pounds, 10 shillings. Class, 19th. Minister's money, 11 pence. Dwelling of two stories, yard and small back house." We had established, then, that the James Ward bakery of 1834 had been occupied in 1830 by the Crawfords.

With this much evidence in our possession, we were now fairly certain that we were pursuing the right Crawford family. Looking further into the birth, death, and marriage records of the family, we found additional confirmation. Patrick Robert Crawford, the baker of Bow Lane, had married Ann Crawford. These two were Ida's maternal grandparents. They had five children: Ann, born in Dublin on November 20, 1814, who married Thomas Walsh; Eliza, Mary, and Margaret, all Ida's aunts; and Patrick Crawford, her uncle.

Ann and Thomas, of course, were Ida's parents. Ann's sister Mary, two years after her father's death, married the foreman of the bakery, Michael Kennedy; later they moved to another site in Dublin, where they opened a new bakery at 148 Upper Abbey Street under the Kennedy name. We discovered it still occupying that site, and still owned by a Kennedy, Hugh, who verified the fact that his grandmother's name had been Mary Crawford before her mariage to his grandfather Michael. That explained one of the addresses

Ida had left behind her: "Mary Kennedy, 148 Upper Abbey Street."

In the marriage register of St. James Church (Church of Ireland) on James Street in Dublin we found Michael and Mary's marriage recorded on February 25, 1829, with "Pat'k Crawford" (Ida's Uncle Patrick) as one of the witnesses. On the same day, they were married again at the Catholic Church of St. James, virtually around the corner. In the eyes of both contending faiths, they were truly married by the end of that day.

It was Mary's and Michael's son Peter whose photograph I had brought to Ireland. Identification was established by Peter's son, Hugh, the proprietor of the present Kennedy bakery. Hugh had succeeded his father as owner after Peter's death in 1889.

Mary's sister, Margaret, was born July 11 and baptized July 20, 1817, so the records showed, when the register of St. Laurence Church (Church of Ireland), just outside Dublin, was examined. Twenty-two years later at the parish church of Rochdale, Lancashire, England (a subsequent investigation disclosed), she was married to a stonemason named John Connell, of Littleborough. The register once more showed her father as Patrick Crawford, baker, of Dublin.

At some point in the next quarter-century, John Connell died and on March 16, 1864, his widow was married again, to Malachy Larkin. Once again the register showed her parentage: Patrick and Ann Crawford; father's occupation, baker.

When Margaret Larkin and Mary Kennedy died (at

eighty-one and eighty-five respectively) both were buried in the Kennedy plot at Glasnevin Cemetery. Margaret's Summer Hill address which we had found in Ida's scribbled notes was where she went on living after Malachy died in 1878. Ida quite probably had written it down at the time of his passing.

These were the primary limbs on the family tree, but we nevertheless examined as far as we could the existence of other Crawfords in Ireland. We also looked for the presence of Walshes. It appeared that every Walsh family in the country must have had a Thomas, and every Crawford family an Ann. Every Thomas seemed to have a brother John, and every Ann a sister or two.

The number of Thomas Walshes who had married Ann Crawfords was astonishing. Whether they lived in Sligo, in Donegal or in Westmeath, in Kildare or in Meath, or in some other county, they all tried to attach themselves as claimants of Ida's fortune to that single marriage record we found for Ida's parents. Most of them thought no further proof was necessary.

One stubborn fact, in my view, eliminated many of these claimants. We had established to our own satisfaction that Thomas Walsh's mother, Grandmother Margaret Walsh, had died in Malden, Massachusetts, and not in Ireland. Unfortunately for those who claimed through a Thomas Walsh who qualified in other respects, the mother of each of these Thomases had died in Ireland.

Examining some of the claims, we found verification of an odd historical fact. It appeared that when people left Ireland in the 1840's to come to the New World, they did not often choose their own destinations. They simply went where the ship was going. If members of a family left in different ships, they might find themselves scattered in such widely separated places as Newfoundland, Nova Scotia, New England, and New Orleans. Many of those who landed in Canada eventually made their way to the United States.

If there was an abundance of Crawfords and Walshes in Ireland, there was also a number of Mayfields. We knew they existed in profusion in the American Deep South, but now we learned that their Irish ancestors were equally numerous. These Southern Mayfields, we determined, had originated in Ireland, where their ancestors were well-known silversmiths around 1800. Several towns in Ireland are named Mayfield.

Similarly we traced what we could of the Crawford family outside Dublin. Originally from Ayrshire, they could be followed in the records of land transfers through great estates held in several counties, down to smaller ones in other counties. The Crawfords were soldiers, clergymen, civil officials, manufacturers, merchants, and small tradesmen. Some were of the Ascendancy; some were avowed rebels. There were Episcopalians, Presbyterians, and Catholics. A few were very rich; many shared the poverty of the masses.

With the exploration of these interesting but unprofitable side paths, our investigation in Ireland was at an end. I had learned a great deal about the Crawfords in Dublin, enough to establish the key facts which were needed. It was possible to draw a family tree with Patrick and Ann Crawford at its head and their five children spread out below.

Of these children Ann was the most important, of course, because she became Ida's mother, but Ann's sister Eliza, Ida's beloved Aunt Eliza, continued to hold my fascinated interest, and it was her progress which led to our next move.

I remembered the stories of Aunt Eliza her children and grandchildren had told us. Her father, the baker, had been her hero. She had often spoken of him as an upstanding Protestant, a pillar of the church, who entertained the minister in his home.

"I gave the minister a sampler once," Aunt Eliza would tell her children, remembering proudly. "He paid me a great compliment to ask me for it, but to tell you the truth, I'd much rather have kept it for myself. I couldn't, though, because I knew he'd asked me for it out of the great respect he had for Father."

It was this minister who proved to be a fateful influence in Aunt Eliza's life. Dublin was in a religious turmoil as she was growing up. The long struggle for Catholic emancipation was nearing its end, and the controversy was bitter. Even girls as young as Eliza were drawn into it, hearing the conversation of their parents and their friends at school. Eliza's father was positive about what was going to happen if the Catholics won. They would, he said, ruin the country, and the Protestants would lose their dominant position.

Eliza thought about religion a great deal. She wondered what the Catholics were up to, what they really believed, and she tried to persuade some of the Catholic girls she knew to take her to their church, but they were frightened by the mere idea of taking a Protestant into those holy precincts. Then, sitting in her own church one day and listening to her father's friend, the minister, something he said—she never could remember exactly what it was—raised troubling questions in her mind. She *had* to find out what the Catholics believed.

Alone and secretly she went to a Catholic service, then to another, and before long she was taking instructions, hiding the books the priest gave her.

The fact that she was becoming a Catholic filled young Eliza with a sense of excitement and exaltation. It was the greatest secret she had ever known in her life, and she was bursting to tell someone. But she was afraid, too, that when she did her strict Protestant family would disown her.

One night, after she had gone to bed, she could hold her secret no longer, and told her sister Ann, Ida's mother. Ann gave her the strength to confront their father. When he heard the news, Eliza watched the emotions cross his face—amazement and disbelief, then a great sadness, and finally the familiar, stern countenance he displayed when he was at his most inflexible.

Eliza would have to go, he told her. He could not have a Papist under his roof. There would always be money for her if she needed it, but she would have to leave home. Desolate and sobbing, but determined and staunch in her new faith, Eliza packed her few belongings and left.

No one knew exactly where she went. Eliza's grandchild, Katherine Sheehan, who had first told this story to the lawyer in Salem, Massachusetts, supposed, however, that Aunt Eliza had gone directly to England. That was the next place she had talked to Katherine Sheehan about living in, and Mrs. Sheehan remembered it well enough because Aunt Eliza had married there. Eliza always spoke proudly of the fact that her whole family became Catholic eventually, except for her mother, who had died when she was very young, and her father, "who died before I could influence him," as she put it.

In fleeing to England, Aunt Eliza became part of an exodus of Irishmen leaving their country at that time for a different reason. In 1826 the British parliament had brought near ruin upon a part of Ireland by repealing the tariff on textiles entering the country. For more than two hundred years the Irish textile industry had been concentrated in what was known as the Earl of Meath's Liberty, a vast tract once identified with the priory established in honor of Thomas à Becket, the twelfth century English chancellor and Archbishop of Canterbury under Henry II who was later canonized. Repeal of the tariff not only ruined the textile industry, but ruined every business dependent on it.

Patrick Crawford's bakery was one of those businesses. It was entirely dependent on the weavers who were now out of work. Most of them left at once for England, and in 1830 a public subscription was taken up to send the remainder, who had been left destitute. Aunt Eliza's future husband was a part of this migration, and so was Ida's father-to-be.

I could easily picture the determined figure of Eliza, cast out by her stern Protestant father and taking up a new life in England, leaving behind her in Dublin a favorite sister, Ann, the girl who would become Ida's mother. It was only a momentary interruption in the intertwined histories of these two sisters, who were close to each other all their lives. Where one went, the other must follow, and the trail led unswervingly to England, where I would soon be able to complete what I hoped would be an unassailable record we were compiling to establish Ida Wood's identity.

16

I HAD DRAWN a family tree which contained the names of every person who might possibly have any connection with the case. In England there began once more the examination of church records for baptisms or marriages relating to the persons named in the family tree. At Somerset House, in London, I conducted an extensive search through voluminous records, looking constantly for the names of Mayfields, Walshes, and Crawfords, and scrutinizing hundreds of birth, marriage, and death certificates.

After piecing together this evidence, I could pick up once more the story of Eliza Crawford after her banishment from her father's house in Dublin, although the clues at first were meager. I discovered that she had worked as a servant girl in various English homes until she came at last to Leeds, where she met Thomas O'Connor and married him.

Good Catholic that she was, Eliza saw to it that she and Thomas married twice. The promised emancipation had come, but a law validating marriage by a priest of the Catholic Church would not be adopted in England for four more years. Consequently Eliza and Thomas began by breaking the law and getting married in St. Patrick's Catholic Church, Leeds, on March 3, 1832. There were no witnesses listed in the church record; law breakers did not want to get their friends into trouble by making them accessories. Two days later they were married again in the parish (Established) church of Leeds, according to English law.

Eliza and Tom had their first child, Mary Ann, on December 29, 1832, and it was baptized in Manchester where they had moved meantime. Tom was on the move frequently. He was a "licensed hawker," a peddler of textiles, going from one midland city to another. Two years later, while they were still in Manchester, Eliza bore her second child, another girl, Eliza Jane. When the third child, Winifred, was born three years later they were in Huddersfield, Yorkshire.

While the O'Connors were in Manchester, Eliza's sister Ann caught up with her. How and why she came there no one knows. It may be that she left home under much the same circumstances Eliza had, because of religious differences with their father. Possibly she came to Manchester to escape the poverty in Ireland and to be near her sister.

In any case, she was drawn into the O'Connors' circle of friends, one of whom was young Thomas Walsh, another hawker of textiles. Ann and Thomas Walsh fell in love, and were married in Manchester on February 7, 1836.

Ann's first child was born when she had been married less than a year. It was a son named John Redmond Walsh, who was born in Huddersfield, where Ann and her husband Thomas had followed the O'Connors. Three days later Eliza was godmother for John Redmond—the John whom Ida memorialized on the tombstone in Calvary Cemetery in New York among the "infant children gone before."

The O'Connors stayed in Huddersfield, but the Walshes moved on to Oldham, in Lancashire. A hawker in the textile business had to go where the business was, and Tom Walsh's trade compelled the separation of the sisters for a time. In Oldham, Ann had her second child, a girl named Ellen, born in 1838. The infant's godfather was Matthew Fitzpatrick, who was married to her father's sister. This was the Uncle Matthew, it will be recalled, who sold the house in Malden to Ida's Grandmother Walsh, where Ida lived before she left Malden for New York City.

I finally found my way to the church in Oldham. I asked the priest to allow me to examine the original record made at the time of the baptism of Ellen Walsh.

It was an unforgettable moment. Here was the original entry. Here, in the faded book which I held in my hand, was the birth record of Ellen Walsh. The infant born in this rural English community would grow up in America, marry a member of a prominent New York family, invent a new life for herself as Ida Mayfield, taking her family with her into the grand deception which she practiced her whole life long as the wife of Benjamin Wood.

I had penetrated to the heart of the mystery. Many questions remained to be answered, but I had come, I believed, to the hard core of Ida Ellen Walsh Mayfield Wood's identity.

This birth certificate also moved another piece of the jigsaw puzzle into place. "Old La" in Ida's Old Memoranda opposite "E" could only mean "Oldham, Lancashire," and not Louisiana, as some had supposed.

The search for birth records led next to Leeds, where apparently the peripatetic Walshes moved the year after Ellen was born. A second daughter, Elizabeth, was born there in 1839—still another of the "children gone before" identified. Poor little Elizabeth was gone almost immediately; she died that year. But the Walshes were a fertile family, and the following year Ann bore a fourth child, Mary Ann. Another piece in the puzzle. That explained the "Lee York" following the "M" in the Old Memoranda. It was, of course, "Leeds, Yorkshire," and Mary Ann was the girl who later became Mary E. Mayfield.

When the great census of England was taken in 1841—figures which we examined now with special interest—changes had occurred in the lives of the O'Connors and the Walshes. Either Thomas Walsh had fallen upon bad times, or some kind of expediency dictated that the two families share the same house in Huddersfield, to which the Walshes had returned from Leeds in the intervening year.

There they all were: Tom O'Connor and Eliza, and their children Mary Ann, Eliza Jane, Winifred, and Thomas; and with them, Thomas and Ann Walsh, with their two children, Ellen and Mary Ann. Ann had lost both her son John and the infant daughter Elizabeth. And sure enough—the birth dates given for Ellen and Mary Walsh were exactly those in the Old Memoranda for "E" and "M."

The two-family occupancy in Huddersfield was temporary, because the Walshes moved on again to Halifax, England, in 1842, where a fifth child, Eliza, undoubtedly named for her aunt, was born, and unfortunately soon joined the melancholy company of the "infant children gone before."

Some time during the next three years the urge to seek new opportunities elsewhere seems to have driven the O'Connors and the Walshes almost simultaneously. By 1845 the O'Conners were established in Salem and the Walshes in Boston, where Ida's mother Ann continued to give birth to children who failed to live long—no doubt the result of some hereditary weakness, which may also have been responsible for poor Emma's curvature of the spine.

Little Thomas, born in Boston in October, 1845, was only eleven months old when he died. Patrick Danvir's receipt for his burial, it will be recalled, helped to lead to the initial discovery of the Walshes. Another Thomas was born in 1847, but he died before the year was over. Both of these children's names appeared on the Cambridge gravestone, and were among the infants gone before on the Calvary monument.

To the Crawford girls, Eliza and her sister Ann, the Dublin days and people they had known must have seemed remote in the busy New England to which they had migrated from England in the forties. But their lives and fortunes continued to be intimately interwoven. They shared their tragedies and their small successes, and continued to live near each other, while both men carried on the same kind of textile trading they had conducted in England.

A disaster overtook the O'Connors in 1866. Tom had been on a trading trip, and was in Portland, Maine, one night when a fire broke out in the barn behind the inn where he was stopping. Tom rushed out with the others, and saw that it was too late to save the barn. All he could do was try to rescue the trapped horses, which was not only an act of humanity but an effort to salvage his means of livelihood. It was the horses which carried him and his wagon to the farmers with whom he did his trading. In saving the horses, however, Tom O'Connor lost his own life.

His friend Thomas Walsh, Ida's father, had died two years before in San Francisco, as we had learned. That trip to California had been a desperate attempt to make a new start, apparently, since things had gone badly for him in America.

While the two heads of the families were still alive, however, the Walshes and O'Connors were constantly together, as they had been in England. For a time both families were in Salem, and briefly, perhaps during one of Thomas Walsh's bad periods, they lived again in the same house. Michael, the only one of Ann Walsh's male children who lived to grow up, and whose name was changed to Henry Mayfield, was born during this Salem period.

Ellen and her sister Mary were frequent visitors in the O'Connor household, wherever the families might be living. Their Aunt Eliza set aside a room for them to play with *her* Mary, Eliza Jane, and Winifred whenever her husband came home from one of his selling trips, and wanted peace and quiet.

One day the two cousins, Ellen (as it seemed only logical now to call Ida Wood, in this childhood context) and her cousin Eliza Jane had an adventure they talked about for the rest of their lives. Walking in Malden together, they saw a sign in a window: "Your Future and Fortune Told." Giggling excitedly they pooled their money, and discovered they had enough to consult the gypsy seer who presided over the readings. In her dingy parlor, probably more than a little frightened, they stared with fascinated, round eyes at their palms over which the gypsy woman's finger traced the pattern of their future.

"My dear," the clairvoyant assured Ellen, "you are going to be a very lucky girl. You are going to marry a rich man, and get everything you want out of this life. As for you, little one," and she turned to Eliza Jane, "you will not be rich but you will not be unhappy, and you will end your days living in a white house with trees around it."

The girls went home that day buzzing with excitement, and told the other cousins about the gypsy's prophecies. It became a family tradition, and oddly enough, it came true. Nearly forty years later Ida's sister, Mary Ann Walsh, knocked on the door at Eliza Jane's house on Bow Street, Salem, where Aunt Eliza, then approaching the end of her life was living with her daughter. Mary was "dressed like a fine lady," Eliza Jane remembered later, and so many years had gone by that she failed to recognize her cousin.

"Does Mrs. O'Connor live here?" Mary inquired politely.

"Yes, she does," Eliza Jane said, looking at the familiar face before her, and trying hard to place it.

"I'm an old friend of hers, visiting from New York," Mary said, keeping a straight face. "I'd like to say hello to her if she's home."

"Why, yes, come right in," her cousin said, somewhat flustered, and still searching her memory.

Mary sat down in the little formal parlor and waited while Eliza Jane went to get her mother. When Aunt Eliza came in the room hesitantly, peering at her visitor, Mary stood up and said simply, "Don't you remember me, Aunt Eliza? I'm Mary Ann Walsh."

"Is it possible!" Aunt Eliza cried, looked again, and put her arms around Mary, and so did Eliza Jane, who could only say, like her mother, "Is it possible! Is it possible!" They were all in happy tears.

For hours the three sat talking about old times. Aunt Eliza got out the family album, and the women chatted happily over the pictures. One of them was undoubtedly the tintype showing the two sisters, Ida's Aunt Eliza and Ida's mother, Ann, together. It was taken shortly after Ann had learned that her husband Thomas was dead in San Francisco, and she was in widow's weeds.

Not once while she was there did Miss Mary so much as hint at the deception being practiced in New York by herself and her sister Ida. She had introduced herself as Mary Ann Walsh, and when she spoke of Ida, she called her Ellen. There was no mention of the Mayfield name, and in fact Mary did not even disclose that Ellen had become Mrs. Benjamin Wood. There was not the slightest exposure of the fact that the Walshes had been transformed into the sugar aristocracy of Louisiana. Mary was careful not to leave any New York address.

All she told the two Elizas was that Ellen had, indeed, married a rich man, and was happy. They were all happy, she said, and they spoke often of the old days in New England. Glancing around the plain interior of Eliza Jane's home, Mary must have observed that life was not too easy for her relatives, and when she left, she slipped some money into her aunt's hand.

"Ellen will be so happy to hear that you are alive and well," she told Aunt Eliza. "I know she'll want to send you a gift."

Warmhearted Mary probably believed her sister would make such a gesture, or perhaps it was a remark generated by the emotion of the moment. In any case, Aunt Eliza took it with the seriousness of an old lady who has nothing else to do or think about. Mary's visit had been the most exciting moment in her life for years, and the promise of a gift no doubt meant as much as the gift itself. It meant hearing from Ellen again, re-creating a happy time she thought had gone. For the three years remaining to her, Aunt Eliza waited hopefully for the mailman every day. No gift or letter from Ellen ever came.

A year after this visit the family moved from 9 Bow Street, where Mary had called, to another house down the block, at number 15. "The fortune teller was right!" Eliza Jane exclaimed, "Ellen has married her rich man, and here is my white house with trees around it."

When it was her turn to sit in the rocking chair by the window, like her mother, and wait for the days to go by, Ida's cousin Eliza Jane repeated that observation over and over until it became a family saying, another part of the O'Connor-Walsh legend.

Armed with all the material which I had painstakingly gathered and catalogued, I regarded my search as ended. After further long legal research, I was ready to face the trial before Surrogate Foley on the issue of Ida's identity.

In spite of the exhaustive preparation I had made, however, there were some worrisome questions which remained elusively beyond every attempt to resolve them. There was, for example, the question of Emma. The available evidence indicated that she must be Ida's sister, but there existed the nagging doubt that she might really be a daughter. After all, we knew so little of Ida's life before she came to New York. Was it possible that she had fled to the city because she had given birth to Emma?

There was also the question of the Continental Hotel in Philadelphia. This hostelry appeared and reappeared in the history of Ida's life. Cakes of soap from there, it will be recalled, had been found in her effects, and the "Continental

Hotel, Philadelphia, Pennsylvania," was given as Ida's address in the records of the Lincoln Safe Deposit Company where she rented a box. The unconfirmed story, according to Ida's own verbal reminiscences, was that she had met Ben there when she was only fifteen. In 1907, when she, along with Mary and Emma, registered at the Herald Square Hotel, Ida had given her previous address as the Continental. We found it difficult to credit Ida's statement to the nurses that she was fifteen years old when she met Ben, either at the Continental Hotel or anywhere else. The possibility did, however, exist that she met him there several years later. Yet it was a fact that there was no documentary or other evidence in existence which would definitely place either Ida or Ben at that hotel at any time.

Since we knew nothing for certain of Ida's life before she came to New York, the lingering doubt remained that we might have the wrong person. We deduced, but we had no supporting documentary evidence, that Ida came to New York City from Malden. Ida, it will be recalled, was not listed in the 1855 Malden census. The first evidence of her presence in New York came from her bold 1857 letter to Ben.

Following that line of reasoning opened another. Was it possible that there was something in the Mayfield contention after all, and Ida had met Ben in Louisiana? For all we knew she might have been there before she came to New York. As for Ben, it was stated in his obituary published in the *Daily News* that he had been working there as a moss gatherer during the period before Ida's first New York appearance. I also recalled the search I had made for Ida's possible application for naturalization, both in Malden and in New York. I could find none either for Ida or the other members of her family, though it appeared they were born in the British Isles.

As my mind worried over these doubts and possibilities, I had to remind myself of the impressive mass of documentary evidence I had compiled, including the rose-colored notebook and the Old Memoranda, both in Ida's handwriting, which declared that the facts were quite contrary to these speculations. When I did that, I could reassure myself that I was experiencing only the natural qualms lawyers often feel before a trial. But then I would think of the fact that the rose-colored notebook bore the stamp of a New Orleans stationery firm. I also considered the swarm of Louisiana Mayfields, spending so much time and money, and the formidable array of lawyers representing them. Surely (the thought went through my mind) these people must have some reason to believe they have a good case.

In any event, the months and years of investigation and preparation were over, and the day of courtroom battle was at hand. I was ready for it.

17

THE CASE OF IDA WOOD began on a hot, humid day in August, 1937, when the Honorable James A. Foley took his seat on the bench as he had done on numberless other occasions since 1919, when he was elected Surrogate.

The claimants had grown remarkably in number. When Surrogate Foley in 1934 denied probate to Ida's will because the sole beneficiaries, Emma and Mary, had predeceased her, and the signature of one of the two witnesses could not be proved, there had been only about two hundred people claiming various degrees of alleged relationship. But in granting letters of administration to the Public Administrator, the Surrogate had invited anyone asserting relationship to Ida to serve notice of his claim on the Administrator. By the time the Public Administrator filed with the Surrogate on January 7, 1937, the account of his stewardship of Ida's assets, 1,103 persons had filed such notices with him. All of these were given notice of the proceeding. Of this number, 616 appeared by counsel in the proceeding to press their claim of relationship. Each claimant was compelled to file a bill of particulars tracing his relationship up to the common ancestor and then down to Ida.

The case could not have been heard before a more distinguished jurist. Surrogate Foley was a tall and impressive man, with fine features, a high forehead, and an infectious smile that mitigated the dignity of his pince-nez glasses. He was a kind, sympathetic, patient gentleman, who during his service in the court had tried many complicated and important cases. Leading members of the bar frequently appeared before him in estate matters. He had served as New York Assemblyman and State Senator, and had been chairman of the commission to investigate defects in the laws of decedents' estates, commonly referred to as the Foley Commission.

On the bench the Judge was quick and alert, nervous, and on occasion he gave the appearance, at least, of impatience. But his knowledge of the law in this field was extremely wide, and he was looked upon with utmost respect by all the probate judges in the nation. His carefully reasoned, concisely written decisions are still constantly cited by lawyers and judges as authoritative statements of the law.

Surrogate Foley's background and experience as a man of the people qualified him uniquely to be a Surrogate. Affable and kindly off the bench, with a lively interest in current affairs, in court he personified justice and humanitarianism, but he brooked no inattention.

Lawyers who practiced before him regarded the Surrogate as a master of his profession—austere, careful, and thorough, but always polite and never arrogant. When he was hearing arguments on motions, he had a habit of standing behind his chair and actively questioning the lawyers' arguments, a practice risked only by the most confident of judges. While he actively participated in the proceedings before him, he managed to maintain an air of detachment from them, so that litigants or their attorneys were always aware that his role was that of an arbiter in search of justice. He had a phenomenal memory for cases, often recalling the exact volume and page number of an applicable decision. Lawyers preparing motions or cases for trial before Surrogate Foley knew they had better be completely prepared, or they would be embarrassed.

The courtroom over which the Surrogate presided was in the imposing structure known as the Hall of Records. The spacious room was paneled in rich mahogany. The windows looked out at one side on the Chambers Street traffic coming and going to Brooklyn Bridge, and City Hall Park, consequently it was understandable the Surrogate would not permit them to be opened in spite of the heat because the traffic noise and occasional City Hall parades would have drowned out the witnesses.

This mahogany-paneled courtroom seemed to epitomize justice, elegance, and tradition. Three huge crystal chandeliers which hung from a gold-leafed high ceiling cast just enough light to add a certain dignity to the proceedings, while at each side of the room enormous rose-pink marble fireplaces lent warmth to the scene.

Ida, in death, had drawn an overflow crowd to the final act of the drama that was her life. The courtroom was filled, and some spectators had to sit on the steps leading to the gallery. Many interested people could not get in at all, and lined the corridors outside. Inside, Judge Foley had posted three court attendants to maintain order, and reminded them that he would not permit the slightest sound to enter the court if the doors leading outside had to be opened.

The long counsel table itself was too small to accommodate

all the numerous attorneys present. At my side was my energetic, hard-working associate, Joseph Arenson, who had spent countless hours with me working on the case, and who had been ready at any time for any task I might assign to him.

Next to Arenson sat Martin Conboy, a veteran of the bar whose reputation as a trial lawyer ranked with that of such noted figures as Max Steuer, Theodore Kiendl, and John Stanchfield. At that time he was in his middle fifties, about six feet tall, a man of formidable dignity. He was a portly gentleman with a ruddy, kind face and a quiet manner, whose piercing gray-blue eyes appeared to search out the truth in everyone. He was representing some of the Walsh claimants.

Conboy was being assisted by his associate, Thomas J. Nevins, a methodical, hard-working attorney of great ability, who had begun his successful legal career as an assistant to Conboy in the office of the O'Brien firm.

Other Walsh claimants were represented by Edward T. Corcoran. It will be recalled that he had acted as Ida's Special Guardian in her incompetency proceeding. Later he was retained as attorney by several of the Walsh claimants to advance their interests.

Henry Uterhart represented many of the Mayfields—a tall, gangling, awkward man, with a slow, drawling, somewhat monotonous voice, often referred to as a society lawyer. He would begin sentences in the middle and conclude them in the middle, jumping from one thought to another with extraordinary agility, and without completing any of them. He tended at times to ask "leading questions" on direct examination of his own witnesses, that is, questions that suggested desired answers. Surrogate Foley frequently cautioned him on this subject.

James Madison Blackwell also represented a number of the Mayfield claimants. A man of medium height, he spoke with a well-modulated voice, and was courteous in his demeanor not only to the court but to opposing counsel. An able lawyer, he was persistent in pressing a point when he believed it was given insufficient recognition.

These were the principal actors in the courtroom drama, but there were many other lawyers present, each representing anywhere from one to fifty claimants. There were so many lawyers that Surrogate Foley directed the Clerk at the outset of the hearing to "call the roll" of the attorneys present. Because of the lack of space at the counsel table, many of these lawyers and their assistants had to sit on the chairs usually reserved for prospective witnesses or for the public.

The first trial before the Surrogate, according to the procedure he had laid down, was to determine who was the closest to Ida through her husband. The dispute between the two Wood factions had been raging for some time. The rumors that Ben had married not only a Catherine Davidson but also a Delia Watts were still heard. Now they were to be put to rest finally by the requirements of judicial proof. This showed that Ben had married only Catherine Davidson, who died before he married Ida.

Two sons, Benjamin, Jr., and Henry, were born of this marriage. Benjamin, Jr., died without leaving issue. The Blanche Wood Shields faction was composed of the children and grandchildren of Ben's son Henry. These facts found by the Surrogate confirmed his decision five years earlier when he granted temporary letters of administration to a representative of this faction when Ida's 1889 will was offered for probate.

The Surrogate ruled that five Wood descendants—Gertrude A., Henry, and Howard S. Wood, Blanche Wood Shields and Mabel Wood Russ—were the nearest and next of kin to Ben Wood as his direct descendants. Gertrude and Blanche were Ben's grandchildren, the daughters of his son Henry, or, as the Surrogate stated, "relations in the second degree." Howard, Henry, and Mabel were great-grandchildren of Ben, grandchildren of Ben's son Henry. As such, the Surrogate held, each of the three "are of the third degree of kinship."

By this decision alone the court eliminated seventy-four Wood claimants more remotely related to Ben, such as nephews and nieces, including Otis, grandnieces and grandnephews, and with them their numerous lawyers. The five Woods who remained would be entitled to Ida's estate only if it were determined that she had left no blood relatives.

With that matter disposed of, the court turned to the next issue, which was the crucial one in the whole incredible affair: The proof in court of Ida's identity through her parents, and the establishment of her maiden name. This was the inquiry which would ultimately determine whether or not she had left any blood relatives.

It was the moment when our years of painstaking careful investigation would bear fruit at last, if they were ever to do so.

It was also the moment when the Mayfields and any other prospective heirs would have their day in court. The contentions of the Walsh and Mayfield claimants, as the Surrogate pointed out, were in "absolute and irreconcilable conflict."

18

IN PRESENTING MY CASE that Ida was a Walsh, not a Mayfield, I was not acting as attorney for any claimant to her fortune. I was neutral, reporting to the court the results of my investigation as counsel to the Public Administrator. Corcoran and Conboy represented the Walsh descendants, consequently at this time their interests coincided with what I was about to prove.

After the Public Administrator had been appointed to take charge of Ida's estate, the temporary administrators had turned over to him all of Ida's effects which they had in their possession. These administrators, it will be recalled, were Ben's great-grandson, Henry Wood, and the Bankers Trust Company. They were appointed shortly after Ida's 1889 will was offered for probate. Otis Wood, who had been Ida's committee before that time, during her period of incompetency, had turned over to them the effects which were in his charge.

I made all of these effects available to the various claimants and their attorneys. They could read them in my office, and were free to obtain photostats of any document. I was available to answer questions about them. Before the hearing, I prepared a list of all the papers and documents in my possession, both those found in Ida's effects and those resulting from my other investigations, and distributed it to the claimants and their lawyers. The Mayfield attorneys, including Uterhart and Blackwell, had as much free access to these results as the Walsh attorneys.

The proof of Ida's identity which I presented was largely documentary. These documents—I called them my "silent witnesses"—were among the end results of three years of searching for Ida's identity. I offered the documents in evidence under the so-called pedigree exception to the rule against hearsay evidence. For the benefit of nonlawyers, it may be helpful for me to clarify the rule of evidence known as the "pedigree hearsay exception," which controls proof in court of lineage, descent, and succession of families.

Pedigree is the history of a family transmitted from one generation to the other, down through the ages, and embraces matters relating to kinship, descent, birth, marriage, and death. The "pedigree hearsay exception" proved to be an important feature of the Ida Wood case. There were many documents or statements of witnesses offered in evidence by the attorneys at the hearing which the Surrogate either received in evidence or rejected, depending upon whether they met the requirements of the "pedigree hearsay exception."

It is a well-established rule of evidence in a lawsuit that the testimony of a witness must be based on his own personal knowledge. Hearsay testimony is not admissible because it is not based on the personal knowledge of the witness but upon statements he heard somebody else make. Such testimony has no value because it does not reflect the credibility of the witness but of someone else who is not in court, and therefore is not available to be cross-examined by the opposing party or his attorney.

There are, however, certain exceptions to the admission of hearsay testimony. One of these has to do with cases involving pedigree. If certain requirements or safeguards are met, a pedigree hearsay declaration is admissible in evidence notwithstanding its hearsay character. These requirements are three in number.

First, it must appear that the declarant, that is, the person whose statement is being repeated by the witness, is no longer alive.

Second, the statement or declaration must have been made *ante litem motam,* a Latin expression meaning before the litigation was started or the controversy arose. The purpose of this requirement lies in the greater assurance that a declaration is normally more trustworthy if it was made at a time when there was no motive or temptation to distort the truth.

Third, it must appear that the declarant was related by blood or affinity, that is, by marriage or some close ties, to the family about which the pedigree declaration is made. This relationship, it should be stressed, must be established by independent proof and not by the declaration or statement itself.

Pedigree hearsay declarations may take a great variety of forms, such as entries in family Bibles by a deceased parent or relative, church records of baptisms, marriages, or deaths; cemetery records or inscriptions on tombstones; statements made in opening bank accounts, statements in deeds, letters, oral statements, statements made in court records, such as a petition for probate of a will or an application for letters of administration.

In order for the pedigree hearsay testimony to be admissible, the statement must be of a fact and not an expression of opinion, such as that John Smith must have been related to Mary Jones because they lived in the same house.

The weight to be given by the court to the declaration depends upon the nature of the declaration and the probability of its truth.

At the outset of the documentary proof which I offered in evidence at the Ida Wood hearing, there were the death certificates. They showed the dates of death of Ida; of Mary A. Mayfield, whom I claimed to be Ida's sister; of Ida's alleged daughter, Emma Wood; of Ida's husband, Ben; of her brother, Henry B. Mayfield; and of her mother, Mary Elizabeth Mayfield.

Here, in death, were Ida and the members of her immediate family who lived with her in New York. On October 11, 1883, she had purchased for a thousand dollars a plot large enough to contain sixteen graves, at the Calvary Cemetery in Queens, New York. I proved this through the records regularly kept by the cemetery, which also showed the burial of Ida and each of the other members of the family whose death certificates I had presented.

Ida's mother, it will be recalled, had died in Glasgow, Scotland. From the files of New York City's Department of Health, I offered in evidence the "transit application" for permission to pass her remains through the city, to be buried in Calvary Cemetery. There, as I proved from the records of the cemetery, she was placed in a receiving vault, and thereafter buried in Ida's family plot.

Conboy brought out, through writings found in Ida's effects, which were received in evidence, that both Ben and

Ida participated in negotiations with an Anthony Goldner during 1884 and 1885 for the preparation and lettering of the tombstone. A communication to Goldner in Ida's handwriting showed that she counted the lettering to appear on the monument.

The Mayfield attorneys had thus far offered no objections to the evidence which had been produced. That was understandable, since Ida and her family had died as Woods or Mayfields. Not once was the name Walsh mentioned in the death certificates. There were, to be sure, a few disquieting facts stated in these certificates. For instance, Mary's declared, obviously upon the basis of information supplied by Ida, that her father, "Thomas Henry Mayfield," and her mother, "Ann Mary Crawford," were born in Ireland. Her sister Ida's certificate carried similar information, copied from Mary's certificate, and Ida and Mary's mother was described as "Mary Elizabeth Mayfield, widow of Henry Mayfield, sugar planter."

A death certificate may be received in evidence for the limited purpose of proving the fact of death and the date of death. Everything else, including the statements in the death certificates as to the relationship of Ida, Mary, and the "widow of Henry Mayfield, sugar planter," was excluded as hearsay, since the person who supplied the information for the death certificate was not present in court to testify as to his own personal knowledge of the facts. The rule excluding this other information as hearsay will be seen to make sense when it is recalled that Ida's and Mary's death certificates contained the inaccurate statement that they were born in the United States. Both were born in England.

Much of the evidence I intended to introduce consisted

of written notations or statements made by Ida, and some others by Ben, in their own handwriting, which required a standard of comparison for proving that it was, in fact, their handwriting. For this purpose I introduced Ida's 1889 will, which she herself had written and signed, and which Ben signed as a witness. The Mayfield attorneys could offer no valid objection to this. It will be recalled that Surrogate Foley, while rejecting the will when it was offered for probate in 1934, had established as authentic the signatures of Ben and Ida.

Next I offered in evidence Ida's rose-colored notebook, written in her own hand. The Mayfield attorneys passed the notebook among themselves, their quizzical expressions indicating they did not know quite what to do about this important document in which Ida acknowledged that her mother had died in Glasgow, her father in California, and her brother Henry in New York. Also, the names, dates, and places in it were substantially identical with those given in the death certificates of her mother Mary and her brother Henry, both of whom were buried in Calvary Cemetery in New York.

The notebook was received in evidence over the strenuous objection of the Mayfield attorneys. It established a valuable link to the independent documentary evidence which the death certificates, the Calvary Cemetery records, and the cemetery headstone supplied.

Now I was ready to introduce, confirming Ida's statement about her father's death in California, the receipt found in Ida's effects, given by a Robert E. Kenna to Mother Russell for Ida's father's burial. Again the Mayfield attorneys passed the receipt from one to the other, discussed it in hushed voices, then objected to its introduction. Surrogate Foley received it in evidence, however, as an "ancient document."

I should explain that a document is not normally admissible in evidence unless its due execution can be proved. The law recognizes, however, that this requirement is impossible or impractical as to old documents (that is, documents at least thirty years old) because the writer of the document may be dead or his whereabouts unknown. If it is shown that the document has been in proper custody during the period of its existence, and there is nothing suspicious about its appearance, a document shown to be more than thirty years old may be received in evidence without proof as to its due execution. Proof of proper custody is highly important.

I could not prove the execution of this receipt by Kenna because he was dead. But Surrogate Foley took note of the date of the receipt, November 9, 1864, its aged appearance, and the fact that it was found in Ida's effects, and admitted it.

When this and all the other independent documentary evidence were considered, the Surrogate had a right, I believed, to infer that Ida was a daughter of Thomas Walsh, and that she was a Walsh, not a Mayfield.

The family, including Ida, whose members were buried in Calvary, also lived in New York. By introducing the 1880 census, I was able to show that "Mary E. Mayfield" was listed as head of the household, with Ida, Mary, and Henry as her children, Emma as her granddaughter, and Ben as her son-in-law. The census record showed that the family then lived at 175 West Eleventh Street, with other members of the household listed as Catherine Gleason, servant, and Delia Watts, servant.

Ten years earlier, in the 1870 census, which I also introduced, the family lived at 45 Fifth Avenue. Its only members then were Ida, Ben, his two sons Henry and Benjamin, and Emma his daughter. Delia Watson was also listed as a member of the household.

From the records of the Church of St. Paul the Apostle in New York, I obtained and offered in evidence the marriage certificate of Ida and Ben. Ida was listed as Ida Ellen Walsh Mayfield. Here, then, was Ellen Walsh referring to herself at least in part as Ellen Walsh.

The Mayfield attorneys strongly objected to the documentary evidence I now offered—the letter from Father Young, who had officiated at the wedding, to Father Preston at the Chancery Office in New York, in which he had recorded the dispensation for the mixed marriage.

For seventy years this letter had rested in the Chancery Office, where it had been sent by Father Young in the regular course of church affairs. Its significance lay in Father Young's dropping the name Mayfield in describing Ida as "Ida Ellen Walsh."

The documentary evidence I had offered raised a clear inference, I believed, that Ida, her sister Mary, and her mother were actively engaged in efforts to conceal their origin and identity. If there was any doubt about it, I offered the series of bewildering real property transactions relating to the Williamsburg, Brooklyn, property in which, among other things, Mary as "Walsh" sold the property to herself as "Mayfield" for one dollar, the evident purpose of which was to conceal the Walsh origin of Ida's sister Mary.

There was now proof in the record that Ida was the daughter of Thomas Walsh, that Mary and Emma, according to the records of their births, were Ida's sisters, and that "Mary Elizabeth Walsh Mayfield" was her mother. For the purpose of confirming this and showing the true maiden name of Ida's mother by documentary proof, I offered in evidence a photographic copy of the entry in the marriage registry showing the marriage of Thomas Walsh to Ann Crawford in the County of Lancaster, England, on February 13, 1836.

I now proceeded to introduce in evidence the burial receipt from Patrick Danvir to Thomas Walsh, dated Charlestown (Massachusetts) September 13, 1846. This vital link found in Ida's effects was in reality a twofold document. First, it was in the nature of a deed given for a "family grave in Cambridge" in consideration of the sum of $6. Secondly, it was an acknowledgment of payment of $2.25 "for burying your son & digging grave." On the left side of the receipt was the following notation: "G. 14 R 1 East." The receipt was received in evidence as an ancient document in view of its appearance and age, and the proof that it was found in Ida's custody.

Next I offered the death certificate of Lewis Welch, and I called to the court's attention the confirming notation in Ida's rose-colored notebook: "Louis died May 21. Buried May 23, 1865."

Through the testimony of Frank J. Munyon, superintendent of the Cambridge Catholic Cemetery, whom I called as a witness, it was established that Danvir was a superintendent of the cemetery, that the so-called receipt was a deed to the grave, that the cryptic "G. 14 R 1 East" stood for Grave 14, Range 1, on the east side of the cemetery, and the records showed an infant Thomas Walsh was buried in the grave in September, 1846. Munyon also described the tombstone on the site, and a photograph of it was received in evidence as a pedigree declaration.

The Walsh attorneys carried on the proof of Ida's identity as a Walsh. Corcoran called as witnesses Margaret Armbrust and Isabel Johnstone, two of the nurses who attended her after Ida had been adjudged an incompetent. Their testimony related to statements made to them by Ida about her family.

The nurses' testimony was objected to by the Mayfield attorneys on the ground that what Ida said after she was adjudged an incompetent had no probative value. It appeared from nurse Armbrust's testimony that Ida was feeble and often highly excited. But both nurses reported that when she talked about her family she was calm and friendly.

Surrogate Foley overruled the objection to the nurses' testimony, stating that under established law the testimony was admissible, although the Surrogate declared: "It is for the court to decide whether what she said were statements of fact or simply the ramblings of an incompetent."

I objected to the testimony of the two nurses upon the ground that what Ida said to them was a privileged, confidential communication which related to a matter under continued medical investigation, to wit, her mental status or condition. Surrogate Foley overruled my objection, however, and I have therefore felt free in earlier pages of this book to relate what Ida said to the nurses, as recorded by them, particularly what she said about her family. "Ida," nurse Armbrust testified, "liked to talk about her family." Some of the things she said helped us in our investigation; other things she said proved inaccurate.

My belief has always been that Ida was not speaking the truth when she told the nurses that her father had left for California in disgrace because of an indiscretion. All the evidence indicated that he left to find promising employment so he could send for his family to start a new and better life. Ida had said to the nurses that her mother obtained a divorce from her father, but I was unable to find a record of any divorce, and I do not believe one was obtained. It will be remembered that the first words of the inscription on the tombstone in the Catholic Cemetery in Cambridge were these: "Erected by Ann Walsh in memory of her husband Thomas Walsh who died in San Francisco Nov. 8, 1864, aged 54 years."

Shortly before he departed, Thomas Walsh conveyed the deed to a parcel of property in Malden to his daughter Mary, Ida's sister, on June 17, 1862; Conboy offered the deed in evidence.

Ida's statement about her father was not without purpose. It fitted in with another statement she occasionally made to the nurses, that her mother changed the family name from Walsh to Mayfield because of what her father had done. I did not believe this declaration any more than the other, although quite possibly Ida had come to believe both of them. They shifted responsibility for what she had done from herself to her mother, but I am convinced the responsibility was hers alone. She changed her name to Mayfield as easily as to Mrs. Harvey when it suited her purposes. Ida, and no one else, was the leading actress in the drama.

The nurses testified to statements made by Ida which they did not record. When I later taxed them with this during an intermission in the hearing, they said they didn't think it was important at the time, but they assured me their testimony was the truth. I believed them.

Ida complained to the nurses: "Everything that I have guarded all my life, my money was in safekeeping, and here they are putting it in the banks and the banks will only lose it for me." Occasionally she would call one of the nurses or the other to sit beside her. "I was good-looking," she said on one of these occasions. "I was considered very good-looking at one time."

The hearing proceeded with the introduction in evidence of the inscription intended for Ida's mother's monument, bearing the names of her children and those infants "gone before." "My comment," Corcoran added, "is that the first of this inscription, the first three lines, 'Sacred to the Memory of our Beloved Mother Ann Mary Crawford Mayfield,' appears to be the inscription that still exists on the stone in Calvary Cemetery."

In confirmation of Ida's written notation, Elizabeth's birth certificate was also introduced, showing her father to be Thomas Walsh and her mother Ann Walsh, formerly Crawford, both residing at 3 Lydia Street, London, England. Elizabeth, as her death certificate showed, died when she was eleven months old.

As a foundation for subsequent documentary evidence, Corcoran introduced Ben's 1887 letter to Father Young, in which Ben acknowledged that Emma was Ida's sister, and also Emma's birth certificate, showing her to be born in Malden as the daughter of Thomas and Ann Welch.

This evidence was not received without objection from the

Mayfield attorneys who pointed out, quite correctly, that Ida and particularly Ben had proclaimed Emma to be their daughter in innumerable writings. The Mayfield case, it was made clear, would include an attempt to show that Emma was Ida's illegitimate daughter, not her sister.

Next there was introduced the Malden census of 1855, showing that the Walsh household consisted of Thomas and Ann, the parents, and their children, Mary, the Michael who later became Henry, and Lewis. Next came the Malden census of 1865, showing Ann Welch as a widow, with her children Emma and Lewis. This was a year after Thomas Walsh's death in San Francisco, and six days before Lewis's drowning. Ida's sister Mary had apparently left Malden to join her sister in New York.

At last the Old Memoranda were received in evidence and deciphered for the court. Their importance to our case was that Ida, in her own handwriting, recorded her birth and the births of her brothers and sisters, Michael, Louis, Mary, and Emma.

Throughout the hearing Surrogate Foley had indicated that writings in Ida's hand had great weight in evidence, even more so when they and their contents were confirmed by independent documentary evidence. She was not a claimant, the Surrogate said, and her acknowledgment of family relationships was entitled to great weight where the issue related to disposition of her estate.

Not much was known of Ida's paternal grandparents. Almost all the evidence related to her maternal ancestors. Proof of the mother of Thomas Walsh, Ida's paternal grandmother Margaret Walsh, was introduced in evidence at this point in the form of Thomas Walsh's petition in Massachusetts for letters of administration on his mother's estate.

The next document related to the period when Ida was known as Mrs. Harvey. It was the deed to a parcel of property on West Fifty-fourth Street which she had sold shortly after her marriage to Ben. In it she had referred to herself as Ida E. Wood, formerly Ida Harvey. She had been obliged to describe herself in this way because the deed by which she had purchased the property three years earlier had referred to her as Ida Harvey.

We were ready now to introduce in evidence the birth certificates of the principal characters, both those who participated in the grand impersonation and those who were related to the impersonators. We had, successfully we believed, shown the relationship of Ida to the other members of the Mayfield family, exposed the Mayfield masquerade, broken it down to its Walsh components, established Ida's Walsh and Crawford antecedents, buttressing our case in all instances with Ida's own written statements and independent supporting documentary evidence. Now from Ireland and the British Isles we presented to the court the authenticated birth or baptism records of Ellen-Ida and her sister Mary, her parents Thomas and Ann Crawford Walsh, her paternal grandmother Margaret Walsh, her maternal grandparents Patrick and Ann Crawford. Among the American birth or baptismal certificates received in evidence were those of Michael-Henry, Louis, and of course, Emma. The date and place of each person's birth fitted into the family history and the known life experience of each person in the family.

Now the case was complete, establishing Ida's identity, her maiden name and the identity of her parents. There could be no doubt, we believed, that Ida was Ellen Walsh, the daughter of Thomas Walsh and Ann Crawford Walsh, the maternal granddaughter of Patrick and Ann Crawford.

We awaited the Mayfield case. The quickened activity and excitement at the tables where the Mayfield attorneys sat showed that they were ready, even impatient, to tell their sharply different side of the story.

19

The Mayfields were a highly colorful element in the proceedings. Hundreds of them crowded into the courtroom, some unable to make the transition from the bayous to the city, and consequently carrying their shoes in their hands.

All kinds of rumors, never verified, had been circulating about this gathering of the Mayfield clan in New York. It was said there were so many they had formed a Mayfield Club. Those who could not come sent pleading letters, many asking frankly for a part of the estate because they were in dire poverty, or they wanted to buy a house, or needed the money to pay off a mortgage. These people wrote in the most intimate detail about their troubles.

For a time the courtroom was thick with Southern accents and tales of the old days in Louisiana when Ida Mayfield was supposedly growing up on the old plantation, and other tales of life in New Orleans when Ida and Ben Wood were the bright lights of ante-bellum society in the Cresent City.

The Mayfield attorneys conceded the existence of all the Walshes whom we had documented, but they argued that Ida herself was not a Walsh.

The contention of the Mayfield attorneys, which they stated at the beginning of their case as an introduction to the offering of supporting evidence, began with the proposition that Ida was the daughter of Thomas Henry Mayfield and Mary Ann Crawford, of St. Tammany Parish, Louisiana, in the town of Ponchatoula, about forty miles from New Orleans. As a young girl, they argued, Ida had met Benjamin Wood in Louisiana before the Civil War, while Ben was working as an obscure gatherer of Spanish moss.

"She got into trouble with him," so the argument ran, and subsequently came North in his company, living with her lover as his wife, and eventually marrying him "at least in 1867." Emma was their child, born probably before the marriage. Ida had her baby in Malden, the Mayfield attorneys said, and registered her as Emma Walsh, the name of a family which had once befriended her. At the same time, Ida, who was a Baptist, became a Catholic.

The father of the Walsh family in Malden which had presumably been Ida's benefactor later went to the West Coast and died. His widow, Mary A. Walsh, kept the family in Malden until 1865, when their child Lewis died, after which they came to New York and lived with Ida, who embraced the Walsh daughter, Mary Elizabeth, as a sister and Mary A. Walsh as her mother. The Walshes, in turn, adopted Ida's name, Mayfield.

Twelve witnesses appeared to support the claim that Ida had always been a Mayfield. The first, Gillam Harris, who came from "down in Louisiana," as he testified, had been born a slave, taking his master's name after the Emancipation. Harris said he had been told he was born in Richmond, Virginia, in 1850, which would have made him about eighty-seven years old. He recalled the Civil War clearly—"the fighting, the guns"—and he saw the Union troops who came to liberate him. He had known an Ida Mayfield who lived "on the Chappapella Creek," in Ponchatoula, where he understood she worked as a servant or waitress in a boardinghouse run by a Mrs. Reams, meanwhile living with her sister Mandy Joiner and her husband.

For a period of three or four years in the late sixties, Harris testified, Ida occasionally "passed the place" where he lived, and sometimes attended community dances where he "played the fiddle." A man named Wood accompanied her to some of these dances, but Harris could not say whether Ida was married to him, and there was no one in town he knew or believed to be Ida's mother or father.

Isaac Pierre, the second witness, had also been born a slave. He was unable to read or write, and could only guess how old he was, although he finally ventured that he thought he might have been born about 1856 or 1857. "I've been here a long time," he said, "and the first language I learned was when I was a creo [Creole] boy," a fact confirmed by the soft Cajun accents of his voice.

He had been raised in Chappapella, Pierre testified, and he remembered that a Miss Ida Mayfield had stayed one or two days at his former master's house, where Pierre's mother was employed as a cook. Ida contemplated hiring her, but for some reason she did not give her the job. At that time, shortly after the Civil War, Pierre was about eight years old, and his mother was a cook at a sawmill near New Orleans.

About ten years later, Pierre said, he saw Ida again, this time on a farm owned by a man named John A. Morris, where Pierre worked as a laborer. It must have been ten years later, he said, because he was about eighteen years old, "knocking around with girls, walking with young ladies." He was told that Miss Ida Mayfield had a man named Woods, and he heard her referred to as "Mrs. Woods." He assumed it was this Woods who accompanied Ida on her visit to the farm, and stayed there with her.

A lottery was going on at the time, and in an effort to connect the Ida Mayfield known to Pierre with the Ida E. Wood who died at the Herald Square Hotel, attorney Blackwell sought, but without success, to introduce two documents in evidence. One was a book titled *The History of New Orleans,* which referred to the fact that a Ben Wood and a John A. Morris had been in business together in New Orleans. The second document was also a book, *The Old Merchants of New York City,* in which there was a reference to a Ben Wood who was both a policy dealer and a lottery vendor, although it did not further identify him. Since the real Ben Wood had been involved in both occupations, the inference of the Mayfield attorneys was that Ben had been in Louisiana on lottery business at the time Pierre testified he saw them.

The third witness was Thomas M. Mayfield, of Bogalusa, Louisiana, another elderly man, eighty-six years old, feeble and infirm. His father's name was Thomas Owens Mayfield, he said, and his grandfather on his father's side was called John Henry Mayfield, whose wife's maiden name was Sarah Ann Crawford—or as he put it, "I think my grandmother was Sarah Ann Crawford, if I don't mistake." His grandparents lived in Tangapihoa Parish, Louisiana, near St. Tammany Parish. They had six children: Thomas's father, and five daughters, Jane, Mary Ann, Mandy, Martha and Ida. Thus Thomas claimed to be a nephew of Ida through his father Thomas Owens Mayfield.

All these daughters lived in the same vicinity on Chappapella Creek, "on the Tangapihoa River," about six miles from Ponchatoula. Mary Ann married a man named Jack Lane; Amanda married one called Joiner; one of the other girls married a Henry Coltmeyer.

The Mayfield lawyers produced in evidence a certified copy of a license showing the marriage of Amanda M. Mayfield to Louis Joiner at Covington, Louisiana, on December 29, 1855. The marriage certificate of Mary Ann Mayfield was also received in evidence, but what was lacking, as Surrogate Foley pointed out, was any documentary evidence to show that Ida was a sister of either Amanda or Mary Ann.

Another flaw in the Mayfield case was Thomas's inability to remember dates. Like the two witnesses before him, he could neither read nor write, and his memory was hazy on the most basic matters. His father had died ten years before at the age of eighty-three, he testified, but if that were so, his father would have been born in 1844 and he himself seven years later. In written objections he had filed with the court before the hearing, however, he had said his father died in 1906—thirty-one, not ten, years before the hearing date. He did not know when his aunts were born, although he thought Aunt Jane was the oldest.

Thomas volunteered further that he had known Ida, but this testimony was stricken on the ground that he was a claimant to part of the estate, hence financially interested. In striking the testimony, Surrogate Foley noted: "Under our law no person is permitted to testify to personal transactions with the owner of an estate against whom he is claiming financially. The lips of one person are sealed by death. The law seals the lips of the survivor."

No records of births or deaths were offered in evidence. Thomas' grandparents had died before Thomas was born, and he had never heard any discussions or declarations in his family about who Ida was.

After Thomas had concluded his testimony, Surrogate Foley turned to Henry Uterhart, one of the Mayfield attorneys, and inquired: "What proof have you got, documentary proof, to show that this woman, Ida Wood, was born Ida Mayfield, and who her parents were?"

Uterhart, in reply, pointed to the many instances in which Ida had identified herself as a Mayfield, but the Surrogate answered that this was not persuasive in view of my contention, buttressed by documentary evidence, that she changed her name from Walsh to Mayfield, as the Surrogate put it, "for society pretensions or some other reason, trying to make herself an important person after she married into a famous family in New York." The Surrogate assured Uterhart, however, that his mind was still open.

Next to the stand came Mrs. Daisy Mayfield Weisler, fifty-six years old, born in Canton, Mississippi. She testified that she was the daughter of Isaac Newton Mayfield and Elizabeth Marshall Mayfield, and that the name Mayfield came from both her father's and mother's side because her grandmother on her mother's side was a Mayfield. Mrs. Weisler's father Isaac was born in Canton, Mississippi, she said, and her paternal grandfather Israel Price Mayfield was born in "Carolina or Virginia, I don't remember."

About Ida, Mrs. Weisler's memory was better. She testified that her parents had an uncle, Thomas H. Mayfield, whom they called "Uncle Henry," for reasons which she did not elaborate. This "Uncle Henry" had a daughter Ida, and her parents told her that Ida had often visited them. They called her Ida Mayfield, and later mentioned that she was married to a Benjamin Wood, and lived in New York City. Both the parents of Mrs. Weisler referred to Ida as their cousin, from whom they frequently received letters. But none of these letters could be produced in court, it turned out, because the house in which Mrs. Weisler had lived with her parents burned down in 1921.

Uterhart asked the witness whether she had seen Ida, spoken to her, or read her alleged letters, but again the objection was raised that she was a claimant financially interested in the estate, and therefore could not testify to a conversation with Ida. Surrogate Foley sustained the objection once more.

Nothing in Mrs. Weisler's testimony had placed Ida in New Orleans. Her testimony tended to place Ida's alleged parents in Mississippi, where presumably they were married. When she finished, Surrogate Foley granted a motion to strike her testimony because it failed to support the claimed relationship to Ida. The omission of evidence of such a claim, the Surrogate said, "tends to throw light upon the suspicious nature of the claim."

Now came a fifth witness, Mrs. Bernice Mayfield Miller, of Lincoln, Illinois, seventy-one years old. Her father's name was Abram Mayfield, she said, and his father's name was Ennis Mayfield. Abram, she said, was involved in politics in Illinois as "mayor, sheriff, state senator, and treasurer."

Mrs. Miller testified that both her father and her mother had told her of visits by Ida Mayfield and her husband. One of these visits had occurred when she, Bernice, was about eight years old. She recalled that her father, a Democrat, had remarked that Ida's husband, Benjamin Wood, was also a Democrat and influential in New York politics. Mrs. Miller's mother had described Ida as "peculiar," but Abram had called Ida his cousin and she had called him "Cousin Abe"—perhaps somewhat confusing to hear in Lincoln, Illinois.

But no independent proof, documentary or otherwise, was offered to show that Mrs. Miller was related to Ida, consequently Surrogate Foley granted my motion to strike her testimony from the record.

At this point Surrogate Foley announced a short recess. I welcomed this break in the proceedings, since I was near exhaustion from concentrating on the testimony that Ida was a Mayfield. As I stood in a corner of the corridor outside the courtroom, I watched the Mayfield lawyers, surrounded by the horde of Mayfield claimants who had been unable to gain admittance to the overcrowded courtroom, anxiously inquiring as to what was going on in the court.

I was impressed by the sincerity of many of these Mayfield claimants, but the evidence which was being offered in court by their lawyers to prove that Ida was a Mayfield did nothing more than confuse me. Each witness seemed to be speaking about a different person. There was no coherence either as to time or place when this phantom female was seen, no documentary links to father, mother, or sisters and brothers.

Why, indeed, I asked myself, didn't Mayfield attorneys Uterhart and Blackwell offer a scrap of connecting documentary or independent proof, such as a birth certificate? Surrogate Foley had already told the lawyers that the testimony as to Ida's alleged Mayfield antecedents would be rejected or, if tentatively received, would be stricken, unless independent connecting proof was adduced. I was bewildered by the confident demeanor of the Mayfield lawyers as they walked through the corridor, turning now to this group and now to that group of anxious Mayfield claimants with words of reassurance, since what was happening in the courtroom hardly justified words of reassurance as to the Mayfield case.

Though I actually tried, I could not visualize the woman described in the Mayfield testimony. The instances testified to were fleeting and disparate, remote and hazy. I was still trying vainly to imagine the alleged Mayfield Ida as a young girl or a grown woman with flesh and blood and dimensions when the court clerk, in a loud voice which caused a momentary hush in the corridor, announced that the hearing was about to be resumed.

A new witness took the stand. He was Robert Lee Mayfield, of Red Top, a town in southwestern Missouri, who testified that his father was Logan Henderson Mayfield, born in Tennessee, and that his grandparents on his father's side were William and Catherine Mayfield. He recalled seeing writing which appeared to be the signature of one Thomas H. Mayfield in an old large-size family Bible belonging to his grandfather William. The writing was on a page near the center of the Bible, between the Old and New Testament.

At first the witness declared he had never heard any talk or conversation in the family circle about Thomas H. Mayfield's identity, but later he testified that his brother, William Caleb, told him he believed this Mayfield was a brother of grandmother Catherine. When Robert went on to name his many Mayfield relatives he created so much confusion that lawyer Uterhart had to beg the court's pardon. "There are so many Mayfields that I may be pardoned for mixing them up once in a while," he said.

As for the Bible in question, Robert said he did not know what had become of it, and believed it was lost. Again, when he had concluded, I moved that this testimony be stricken, and the Surrogate, granting it, remarked curtly: "No connection established. Pedigree statements useless. No association or connection with Ida Wood. No proof that Thomas Henry Mayfield was the father of the decedent."

Robert's nephew, John Henderson Mayfield, of Springfield, Missouri, appeared as the seventh witness and tried, among other things, to explain how the Bible was lost. He had last seen it twenty-five years before, he said, in his father's place, and noted that it bore the name of Thomas H. Mayfield. After his father died, the Bible was taken by his stepmother when she moved to Kansas City. Later he heard that it had been thrown out inadvertently during spring housecleaning. His father, he said, had told him that Thomas Henry Mayfield was the brother of Katie, who married John's great-grandfather William, and John's father had informed him that the Mayfields came originally from Scotland, settling in Louisiana. All this testimony was stricken, on my motion.

A new figure appeared as the eighth witness. He was Henry J. Parish, of Southwest City, Missouri, the husband of Eureka Mayfield, daughter of Fountain Tolbert Mayfield, who in turn was a son of William Mayfield. Parish testified that Katie and William Mayfield were the great-grandparents of his wife. Shortly after his marriage in 1899, he said, he and his bride visited her parents, and in the course of a conversation about the Mayfield family, Parish's father-in-law declared that Ida Wood, accompanied by a little girl, had visited him in the late summer of 1871 or 1872. Ida was his cousin, the father-in-law said, the daughter of uncle Thomas H. Mayfield and the wife of a man named Wood, with whom she lived in New York City.

Parish had brought with him a page from an old Bible which had been kept in his father-in-law's home. On it was written the Mayfield family history, but Parish said it went back no farther than 1850, consequently it did not record Katie or William Mayfield, or William's brother Thomas H., Ida's alleged father. This testimony suffered the fate of all the Mayfield statements which had preceded it, on the ground that it had failed to establish proof of any connection between Parish's wife's family and Ida Wood.

Andrew Murray, the next witness, was born in Tangipahoa Parish, Louisiana. As a young man he had been employed from 1884 to 1886 by John A. Morris, both at his farm, which was known as the "Morris Retreat," and on the steamboat *Cora,* which plied the inland waters from Louisiana northward. Murray testified that he had seen Ida, whom he called both Miss Mayfield and Mrs. Wood, alone at the Morris Retreat and in company with Mr. Wood on the *Cora.* The *Cora* had played a part in saluting a visiting Brazilian man-o'-war, a ceremony in which Ida and her husband, Ben Wood, had participated, according to the testimony. Ida had two sisters, one known as Mrs. Joiner and the other as Mrs. Reed, Murray said. The last time he had seen Ida was at Miss Corine Joiner's wedding in New Orleans. Murray said he was acquainted with the Joiners' son, who was present in court.

Corine's wedding was in 1868, Murray testified, although all the other dates he had mentioned were in the 1880's, a circumstance the Surrogate took into account when he declared he did not believe Murray's testimony, partly because his story was confused and partly because of the witness's poor memory for dates. "I don't believe his story," the Surrogate concluded. "It is unworthy of belief, in my opinion."

Redrick Joiner, that son of Mrs. Joiner whom Murray said he knew, became the tenth witness. A resident of Hammond, Louisiana, Joiner testified that he was the son of Lewis Joiner, who had married Mandy Mayfield. His mother had told him that her father's name was Thomas Henry Mayfield and her mother was Mary Ann Crawford; that her sisters were Sarah Jane, Mary Ann, Martha, and Ida. Joiner identified the Thomas Mayfield who had previously testified as the son of Thomas Mayfield, his mother's brother. His grandmother, Mary Ann Crawford Mayfield, had married again, he said, and "she raised another family by the name of Harper." Early in his testimony, Joiner said, in response to questioning by the Surrogate, that he knew and had lived near Truader Carpenter. Truader, it will be recalled, was the beneficiary under Ida's purported Louisiana will, which the Surrogate had held to be "clearly a forgery."

Questioned further by the Surrogate, Joiner testified that he never tried to obtain his grandmother's marriage certificate, and that he did not know what church she was married in, but he had been told that Ida was born in Chappapella, in Louisiana. He never saw his Aunt Ida, who had gotten into some kind of difficulty or "trouble" with a man when she was only sixteen, and had gone off to New Orleans, never to return. Surrogate Foley struck his testimony, too.

John W. Harper, the eleventh witness, had lived all his life near Ponchatoula, Louisiana. He was the grandson of John Harper, who was Mary Ann Crawford Mayfield's second husband. Harper testified about a conversation he had with his Aunt Sarah J. Mayfield, who had been married twice, first to Henry Collomire, then to a Mr. Arso. His aunt had told him that her father's name was Thomas H. Mayfield, and her mother's maiden name was Mary Ann Crawford, and that she had a sister Ida "who left that section of the country." Harper's aunt did not know where Ida had gone, but she had named her granddaughter after the missing sister.

In his testimony, Harper said he had tried unsuccessfully to obtain birth certificates or registrations, having written to twenty-one chancery clerks without getting a reply. He was unable to find any record of the marriage of Thomas H. Mayfield and Mary Ann Crawford. He produced a page from an old Bible (the Bible itself was not produced) containing the names of the Mayfield family. One space on the page was cut out, and Harper asserted that this was where Ida's name had been. This page, he said, had come from Ben Joiner, Amanda Mayfield's son, who was alive but too old to be at the hearing.

When the page was offered in evidence as an "ancient document," I objected to its admission on the ground that its custody was not proved. Surrogate Foley recognized that fact, but he admitted the page in evidence anyway. However, when Harper had concluded his testimony, the Bible page and his testimony were both stricken, as all the others had been.

The twelfth and last witness was William S. Rownd, who had lived all his life in Hammond, Louisiana. He had been a lawyer for fifty-seven years and a local court judge for six years between 1914–1920. Rownd testified as an expert on Louisiana law, and also described his search for Mayfield records. Before 1900, he said, Louisiana had no Bureau of Vital Statistics and no law requiring births or deaths to be recorded. The recording of statutory marriages had been required since 1875, but marriage was regarded by the Louisiana courts as no more than a civil contract. Most marriages were not statutory, but were made by private contract; consequently, few were recorded.

Rownd described his search for records of Mayfield births, deaths, and marriages in St. Tammany Parish, Tangipahoa Parish and Livingston Parish. He had found no documents except those for the marriage of Lewis Joiner to Amanda (Mandy) Mayfield and Mary Ann Mayfield to John Lang, or Lane. Methodist and Baptist churches kept no records of births and marriages, it appeared; that practice was confined to Episcopal and Roman Catholic churches. No such churches, however, existed in that part of Louisiana at the time of the Civil War or before.

When Rownd declared that he had searched these parishes to find records of the Mayfield family, particularly the marriage of Thomas Mayfield to Mary Ann Crawford, Surrogate Foley inquired why he was looking for the record of this marriage in Louisiana when previous testimony had implied that it occurred in Mississippi. Rownd failed to answer the inquiry. He produced an ancient document, a leather-bound book kept by a Dr. Cohner showing a visit in 1860 to Thomas O. Mayfield to care for his sick son, Thomas, "six years old." The Surrogate refused to admit it because it did not bear on the essential question in the case—the establishing of a connection between Ida Wood and the Louisiana Mayfield claimants.

"There must be thousands of Mayfields and Crawfords all over the South," the Surrogate remarked, just as there were Walshes scattered through Ireland, Australia, and in every part of the United States. We had seen a fair representation of them on the witness stand—Mayfields and their descendants and those who were said to have known them in the old days. They had been a colorful parade, the bent, aged figures of the former slaves who searched the attics of their memories; the polite, soft-spoken Southern small businessmen and their rural cousins, stiff in their city clothes, who recalled from childhood memories the picture of an Ida Wood who may never have existed, or in any case was not the Recluse of Herald Square.

Not one of them had offered any relevant testimony, and no documentary evidence whatever had been produced to show that the Ida Mayfield of Ponchatoula, Louisiana, if she ever existed, was the same person as the Herald Square Ida. No certificate showing the birth of the Louisiana Ida was offered, nor any certificate of marriage of her supposed parents, Thomas Henry Mayfield and Mary Ann Crawford.

As I sat in the hearing room, thinking about the Mayfield contention and the evidence offered in its support, I remembered the introductory statement attorney Blackwell had made at the Surrogate's suggestion. Ida, said Blackwell, had gone to Malden during her time of "trouble," had given birth there to Emma at the home of the Walshes, and later joined them in recognition of their help, and changed their names to Mayfield.

This was the core of the Mayfield claim, but there was not the slightest evidence in the case to support it. No explanation was given or even offered as to how a young girl, Ida, born in a small Louisiana town, came to travel all the way to Malden, Massachusetts, and how she had come to know a family named Walsh living there. Even if one assumed that it was Ben who knew the Walshes, the Mayfield case was barren of supporting proof since it was not shown that Ben was acquainted with the Walshes; indeed, there was nothing in the evidence to indicate that Ben was ever in Malden.

Disproving the claim that Ida was born a Walsh would do the Mayfield claimants little good. That would not prove their case. In such an event it would be held that Ida died without leaving blood relatives, and the relatives of her husband Ben's five grandchildren and great-grandchildren found to be his descendants at the first hearing would inherit Ida's estate.

Apparently the hope of the attorneys for the Mayfield claimants, however, was that the Surrogate would reconsider his rulings if documentary evidence were introduced to show Ida's own representations during her lifetime that she was a Mayfield. There were a good many such representations, of course, containing facts which, so the Mayfield attorneys contended, bolstered the case of their claimants, and weakened the case which had been presented to prove Ida was a Walsh.

One of these was the obituary editorial for Ben which appeared in the *Daily News* on February 28, 1900, which asserted: "Mr. Wood was married twice. His first wife, who died in 1849, bore him two sons, one of whom—Dr. Benjamin Wood of this city—is now living. He was then married on October 25, 1867, to Miss Ida E. W. Mayfield, daughter of Henry T. Mayfield, of Louisiana, and granddaughter of John Robert Crawford. By her he had one daughter—Emma—who, with her mother, survives him. . . . Benjamin Wood entered the arena of active life and self-supporting industry at an early age. All the States, with one exception, that then composed the Union had been visited by him before he had obtained his majority. As supercargo of a trading vessel he had made several voyages to the West Indies and Central America. As one of a company of moss gatherers he had explored the swamps and bayous of Louisiana."

Equally confusing was the letter to Ida, previously quoted, of November, 1888, which began, "Your whole life since your fifteenth year has been in my keeping . . ." and going on to insist that Emma was his and Ida's own daughter.

Kate Moriarty, a retired dressmaker, was called as a witness for the Mayfield claimants. She testified that she had made Emma's "coming-out dress" for her debut in 1891 or 1892, at which time Mary, Ida's sister, told Kate that Emma was eighteen years old. Kate testified further that she had dressed Emma on the night of the ball, observed her in a state of undress, and that the appearance of her body was "youthful and girlish." But we knew that if Emma had died at seventy-one in 1928, her date of birth would be 1857 and she would have been thirty-four or thirty-five years old in 1891 or 1892.

Blanche Wood Shields, Ben's granddaughter, also testified as a witness for the Mayfield claimants. We were surprised when she took the stand. Her purpose, we surmised, was not to prove that Ida was a Mayfield, but to detract from the evidence that she was a Walsh. If she were neither, there would be no blood relatives, and Blanche's group would inherit Ida's estate. Blanche's testimony was that she frequently saw Emma as a child, that Blanche's mother was born in 1851, and "when my mother first met Emma Wood she was just a little child. My mother was old enough to be her mother."

Nevertheless, the documentary evidence of Emma's birthdate was undeniably clear. The certificates of her birth, which I had offered in evidence, showed she was born in Malden on February 10, 1857. That was an impregnable documentary fact, borne out by the Old Memoranda in Ida's handwriting, and fitted into the verified Walsh family facts, including all those stated in the Old Memoranda and in the rose-colored notebook, also in Ida's handwriting.

It seemed clear to me that Emma was under the impression she was Ida's daughter. Only in Ben's letter to Father Young was the supposed fact that she was the sister revealed.

As the hearing drew to a close, I confess I had moments of apprehension, as every lawyer does when he is engaged in the trial of a case. Thinking of the years of work and research I had put into this matter, I was convinced that I had left nothing undone in my preparation. I awaited the Surrogate's decision with a measure of confidence.

I did not have long to wait. No sooner had all the attorneys rested their case than Surrogate Foley announced that he was ready to render his decision.

20

Few judges, even the most experienced and respected, announce their decisions to the litigants and their attorneys immediately after a case is closed. Most judges prefer to reserve decision, and later publish their determination. Surrogate Foley, however, was one of the few who often made a decision known orally from the bench as soon as the case ended. This practice was only partly because of his mastery of the subject matter, or because of his self-confidence on and off the bench. He did it primarily, I believe, because it was part of his temperament and his practice of actively participating in the cases before him.

I was not surprised, then, after our week-long trial was concluded, when he announced his decision and stated his reasons for it. It was 7:25 P.M. when he began to give his decision and nearly 10 o'clock when he finished, but everyone in the hushed courtroom gave him rapt attention.

"The duty cast upon the Surrogate in a case of this kind is a hard one," the Surrogate began, after a few preliminaries. "We observe these claimants in these cases. You gentlemen know, as members of the bar, that I have had several of the most important cases in the course of my service in the past eighteen years. We see these claimants come in hopeful, some of them deluded in the belief they are related to the decedent, some of them distantly related, and yet barred under our statute of inheritance and distribution from participating in the estate because there are others nearer of kin. We see another type, where the evidence is fabricated. With that kind, more drastic treatment must be accorded. It is a very heavy burden put upon the Surrogate as a trial judge to decide these things and decide them honestly and sincerely. . . ."

The Surrogate paused, reaching out for some of the documents that lay on the bench before him in huge disarray. As I glanced about the courtroom, tension was evident in the faces of the lawyers and clients who waited anxiously for his next words.

"The general rule of evidence which applies to a situation of this kind has been frequently stated," Surrogate Foley went on. "Its objective is to lead the court, and the jury where a jury sits with the court, to a reasonable conclusion. That rule is the progressive value of proven coincidences based upon undisputed facts, and all pointing to one conclusion. A single undisputed fact or coincidence may often temporarily point to the truth. Later on, the relevancy of that single fact may be destroyed. In our case, for example, the similarity of the name of the claimant to the decedent, the mere bearing of the name 'Mayfield' by a claimant or the mere bearing of the name 'Crawford' or 'Walsh' or 'Welsh' does not establish that claimant's relationship to Ida Wood. . . .

"What is my feeling at the end of this trial? There is not the slightest doubt in my mind on the documentary evidence in the case—and I reject every bit of oral testimony from consideration for the moment on the side of the Walsh and

Crawford claimants—that Ida E. Wood was born Ellen Walsh."

Relief flooded over me as I heard these words. They carried with them a vindication of my search for Ida Wood, and I remembered again the day I stood in the church in Oldham, England, and stared at the baptismal certificate, the original entry of the birth of Ellen Walsh. The key had turned in the lock that day, and now the door had swung wide open.

"There may have been some variation in the use of her last name," the Surrogate continued. "I cannot reject my own experiences with the interchange of the use of the name 'Walsh' and 'Welsh.' They were confused by people in my early boyhood and in my young manhood in New York, and they are confused today, but the interchange is not of any materiality. Neither is there any doubt in my mind that the father of Ida E. Wood was Thomas Walsh, and that her mother was Ann Crawford."

Up to this point the Surrogate had been delivering his opinion in a solemn, judicial voice, fitting the occasion. Now he sat back in his chair, and in a more reflective mood he gave the reasons for his decision.

"Why," he asked, "is there doubt so entirely eliminated from my consideration of this case? Because of the combination of these undisputed facts which lead to a single conviction. In this situation I will take the testimony of these nurses out. I believe them. I think they told the truth. But as a judge I can disregard their testimony when I consider the other evidence in the case. You have on the Walsh and Crawford claimants' side of the case the established fact that Thomas Walsh and Ann Crawford were married in England. You have the established fact that there was an Ellen Walsh born of that union. You have the established fact of the birth of the other children in sequence.

"There may be little inconsistencies in these census records as we go along, but each new piece of evidence fits in with more convincing force as we compare the lives of these people down through the years from 1836, the date of the marriage of the parents, right down to the date of Ida E. Wood's death. The photographic copy of the register of the marriage of Ida's parents was very convincing to me. There was the signature of Thomas Walsh written just as similarly and resembling in exact degree the signature which he made later, when his mother, Margaret Walsh, died in Massachusetts. The records of the Probate Court present again the signature of this man thirty years later, when we find the family living in Malden, Massachusetts.

"I am not particularly interested as to the whereabouts of Ida in the period of time between 1841, when the census records of England show her residing there, and the time she appears in New York, engaging in certain activities which led to her marriage to Benjamin Wood."

I could not help but smile at these words. Glancing at Conboy and Corcoran, I could see they shared my quiet amusement at the Surrogate's use of the phrase "certain activities" to describe, among other things, the period when Ida was known as "Mrs. Harvey." There also flashed through my mind Ida's enticing letter to Ben shortly after she arrived in New York.

"I am more interested," the Surrogate went on, "in the documentary evidence because, apparently, this woman was very peculiar. We saw the picture, as unfolded in the evidence, that she became a recluse in the last thirty years of her life, but apparently she had that peculiar idea, cloud of secrecy, changing her whereabouts, suppressing her whereabouts, and these elements of character explain the various names she used. Undoubtedly she changed her name from Ellen Walsh to Ida Ellen Walsh, then to Ida E. Harvey, and then to Ida E. Mayfield.

"It is indisputable in this case by the records offered in evidence by the Walsh claimants that she was known as Ida E. Harvey. She described herself as "Mrs. Harvey." It is undisputed that she held property in that name long before there was ever any thought of a fight for the million dollars which she left.

"We also find her known as Mayfield. The census records describe her mother's name as Mayfield about that time. I have said during the trial, and I repeat, that I think this woman had pretensions to a position in society which she felt might not have been realized if she continued to use the name Walsh, or if she had permitted her mother to use the name Walsh, rather than Mayfield. Her motive is clear when it is analyzed by her entrance in the family of the brother of a mayor of New York, and her association and marriage to Benjamin Wood, a man of position and standing. Most of us know the situation in New York City after the Civil War. She changed her name to Mayfield. Mary Mayfield, a sister, assumes that name. Mary, apparently, did not know even how to spell the name she was assuming because she was first known as 'M-a-i-f-e-i-l-d.' In one of the bank records she was even unable to spell the syllable correctly."

By this time Conboy, Corcoran and I seemed to be looking at each other rather than the Surrogate. We were becoming more and more impressed by the Surrogate's mastery of the smallest details of the matter, and we awaited his characterization of the case presented by the Mayfields. Before doing so, however, the Surrogate spoke about Emma, and the support he found for his decision in the statements made by Ida in her own handwriting.

"I have not much impression at the moment," Surrogate Foley said, "as to whether this daughter Emma, the alleged daughter Emma, was the actual daughter of Benjamin Wood or was Ida's sister. It is my belief, however, that she was her sister. But she is a woman of no importance in this case. Her age was probably correctly stated in the death certificate, but certainly her age fits in with the census records and birth records in Massachusetts, which show she was born of Ida Wood's parents. In any event she died before Ida Wood, our decedent, and that fact removes any necessity for actually deciding her exact status.

"I have said that the most impressive testimony in this case, outside of the documentary records, right through is the handwriting notations of Ida Wood herself." Here the Surrogate referred to all the exhibits in the case which were shown to be in Ida's handwriting, and continued: "Any person who would take these records and analyze them, and take the dates and compare them with the proven dates, take Ida Wood's references about her sentiment for her mother, bringing her body here from Glasgow and burying it in a plot owned by Ida Wood, must be convinced that the hypothesis that Ida Wood was a Mayfield, came up here from the South, and took over the family of Walsh, not being related to them by blood, is false and absurd. It is almost preposterous to me as an experienced trial judge."

As the Surrogate went on to discuss the Mayfield contention, I was conscious again that the documentary evidence—my "silent witnesses"—had been the determining factor in the case. My long investigation, often tedious and discouraging, seemed now to be no more than a slight inconvenience compared with the feeling of satisfaction which overwhelmed me as the Surrogate went on with his decision.

"On the Mayfield side of the case," he was saying, "there is not a single document in evidence to show who was the father and mother of Ida Mayfield. If Ida Mayfield was born in Mississippi or Louisiana there is not a single bit of documentary proof to show that Ida was born of those two parents, or that the parents were ever married, and that is a devastating and destructive force against the Mayfield claimants in this case. They may believe there was an Ida Wood or an Ida Mayfield in the family. Maybe there was an Ida Mayfield, but even the page of the Bible offered today had a part of it cut out which couldn't have contained the record of Ida Mayfield in regular sequence, from my observation of family records. I do not believe that the name Ida Mayfield was ever in that paper. It could not have been written there because of the marginal differences of the writing above and below it.

"As I say, it is absurd to think that this woman, Ida Mayfield, or Ida Mayfield Wood, came from the South, found her way into this family in Massachusetts, and would have adopted them, with all the sentiment she shows in her authentic writings for her real family, the Walshes. Furthermore, I do not believe that this Mrs. Crawford, the Southern Mrs. Crawford, ever existed as the actual mother of Ida Mayfield. There is too much sentiment expressed in Ida

Wood's caring for her mother, the bringing of the body of her mother back to the United States, the care she took over the tombstone, the pathetic sentiment in the verse she wrote and had put on the tombstone."

The Surrogate's voice took on its solemn, judicial tone again as he finally disposed of the Mayfield claim: "Upon the whole record I find no evidence whatsoever to sustain the claim of the Mayfield claimants that Ida E. Wood was born Ida Mayfield. Their claims can only be based upon similarity of name. The story about this girl working down in the boardinghouse as a maid or waitress or cook is unbelievable. I have already said I reject as incredible the testimony of the witnesses who testified to the existence of Ida Mayfield in an effort to prove that she was the same person as Ida Wood of New York.

"I stress the marriage certificate, the marriage record of 1867, when Ida was married to Benjamin Wood. She was then known as Ida Ellen Walsh Mayfield, not Ida E. Mayfield. When the notice was sent by the priest, Father Young, to the Chancellor, he used her real name, Ida Ellen Walsh."

Pausing for a moment, the Surrogate looked around the courtroom, and observed the crestfallen Mayfield claimants. Apparently moved to sympathy for their situation, he concluded his decision in a voice filled with compassion: "Now the disappointment of these people who came from the South and spent their money may be great, but they have no legal standing in this court in this case. They never were related to our decedent, Ida E. Wood, and are not presently related."

Surrogate Foley's oral decision was given on August 31,

1937. Two weeks later he issued a written opinion, which was published in Volume 164 of New York Miscellaneous Reports, in which he amplified the reasons for his decision, and cited supporting legal authority. No appeal was taken.

I have often heard it said by surrogates and other judges, both in New York and other states—and I agree—that the written opinion of Surrogate Foley in the Ida Wood case is the leading authority in this country on the law relating to the determination of identity of deceased persons.

The case did not end there, of course. The true claimants to Ida's fortune had to be ascertained. It took almost two years of intensive investigation, and a hearing before Surrogate Foley which consumed four days, to determine the heirs of Ida who were alive when she died. Only those of her heirs who survived her were entitled to the inheritance. On March 17, 1939 Surrogate Foley announced the names of the ten persons who shared equally in Ida's fortune, each of them "first cousins once removed and thereby within the fifth degree of kindred."

Six were the grandchildren of Ida's Aunt Eliza. Three of these—Eugene F. O'Donnell, Thomas Francis O'Donnell, and Katherine J. Sheehan—were the children of Aunt Eliza's daughter Eliza Jane. This was the Eliza Jane, Ida-Ellen's cousin, who had accompanied her on the exciting adventure to the gypsy fortune teller in Malden. Two—Winifred McEneaney and Stephen L. Gallagher—were the children of Eliza's daughter Winifred. The sixth, Thomas F. Reynolds, was the son of Eliza's daughter Emeline. Aunt Eliza's six other children died without issue.

Three—Michael Kennedy, Hugh Kennedy, and Catherine

Kennedy—were the grandchildren of Ida's Aunt Mary who had married Michael Kennedy, the foreman in grandfather Patrick Crawford's Dublin bakery.

The tenth was William F. Murphy, grandson of Ida's Uncle Patrick.

None of those who inherited Ida's fortune had ever met Ida. Indeed, there is no evidence that any of them knew of Ida's existence, except for Mrs. Sheehan, who furnished valuable information in Salem to the O'Brien firm representative about Ida's family background. There was nevertheless justice in the fact that they and not the Mayfields or members of the Blanche Wood Shields group inherited Ida's money. Ida, it will be recalled, "liked to talk about her family," as the nurses testified. The Old Memoranda, the rose-colored notebook, and the host of writings which she safeguarded her whole life long, were dramatic testimony that "her family" were the Walshes and the Crawfords.

But even when the final accounting of Ida's money was made and the inheritances distributed, the strange case had still not been fully solved, except in the legal sense.

Questions persisted. What were Ida's motives in the deception which became her life? How and why had she been able to accomplish the transformation of a whole Walsh family into a family of entirely fictitious Mayfields? There were small inconsistencies, too, and unexplained occurrences. Since they were not susceptible of proof, and had no direct legal bearing on the case, they had not been explored in court.

In retrospect, however, and in possession of all the available evidence which was ever likely to come to light, it was possible now to reconstruct Ellen Walsh's amazing life, and to project it against the background of her family history as well as her known personality.

This reconstruction, as I offer it here, may not explain all the puzzles, but it draws into perspective one of the most incredible hoaxes ever thrust upon a credulous world.

21

To understand the story of Ida Ellen Walsh Mayfield Wood, there is no better place to begin than with her forebears and the times in which they lived. Ellen was a child of those times, and the motivation for her great deception almost certainly originated in what she saw and heard in her early, formative years at home.

Poverty and trouble—these were the dominant themes in her family from the earliest time she could remember. They were the central facts in the life of Ida's paternal grandmother Margaret Walsh, from birth to death. The year 1790, when Margaret was born, was the beginning of long years of turmoil in Ireland. She was eight when rebellion and massacres swept the country, leaving a blood-red trail across the green countryside and through the murky streets of Dublin. Hate and bigotry were the watchwords of the day. Families were riven, old friendships broken, and the terrible specter of famine, always lurking behind the facade of Irish life, threatened Protestant and Catholic, nationalist and pro-British alike. Civil strife added constantly to the dislocation of trade and commerce.

The massacres were no more than over, in 1803, and Margaret was just entering her adolescence, when the Robert

Emmet uprising again overturned the precarious stability which had been achieved at so high a cost.

It was poverty that became the enemy once more in 1826, when tariff protection for Irish textiles was removed, leaving a vast depressed area in Ireland. That, of course, was why the young Irishmen whom Ida's mother Ann and her sister Eliza married were in England instead of their native country. As textile traders, their business had moved across the Irish Sea to the Midlands, where the English textile centers were growing rapidly.

At home in Dublin, violence and the threat of violence were ever-present factors in the lives of every person. As a small child, Ellen had heard her paternal grandmother, Grandmother Walsh, tell the family story of how she had witnessed with her own horrified eyes a man taken from his home, while his wife and children cried out after him, and hanged from his own roofpole while they watched, helpless. That was Edward Molloy, of Rathangen, we had determined.

The hanging, which was only one of many and symptomatic of the violence all about, did tell us, however, something about the atmosphere in which Ellen began to grow up. Edward Molloy's grisly death so impressed itself on Grandmother Walsh that she could never forget it, and in turn she implanted it so indelibly in the receptive consciousness of little Ellen that it was still on her mind shortly before she died, nearly a century later, a hundred and thirty years after the event itself.

From her earliest memories, then, Ellen Walsh knew insecurity, hardship, anxiety, and poverty. No doubt she understood something of hunger, too, and the fear of powerful forces outside her ken which she did not comprehend.

Life was precarious. It made people tough, or it killed them, or in the case of children like Ellen it implanted strangling fears that could not be shaken off in adult life, only submerged and subverted.

Ellen's maternal relatives, the Crawfords, were likewise drawn into the struggle. Her mother Ann was proud of being a Crawford, and she took a proud if no doubt a puzzled view of the fact that the family name could be found written heroically on both sides of the religious conflict. The religious division in the family led to Aunt Eliza's expulsion from her Protestant father's house, and to Ellen's marriage in a Catholic church when she became officially Mrs. Benjamin Wood. Ben was nominally a Protestant. There is no evidence that either one was a particularly religious person, but it was Ellen who had the tradition of Catholicism from her mother and her aunt, and who insisted on the Catholic ceremony, with the necessary dispensation.

Slum conditions in Dublin during the early nineteenth century were among the worst in the world. Ellen heard tales of this squalor from her mother and her Aunt Eliza during the whole time she was growing up. They must have been vivid memories, for the older woman as well as for the child —memories not only of Dublin poverty but of the Black Plague that swept the country for three years. A century afterward, in Salem, Aunt Eliza was still talking about its horror.

Eliza owed her religious conversion to her silent quarrel with the minister's sermon she heard one Sunday, but to this same minister she also owed, along with her sister Ann, Ellen's mother, what little education the girls were able to obtain. He encouraged a school in which girls were taught to sew and make lace, and the baker's daughters went to it. If they missed academic training, they had in its stead a vocational knowledge which may have saved them from an even more difficult time during the first struggling years of their marriages in England. Ann appears in the English census figures as a milliner, and Eliza also made the lace caps she always wore until the end of her days. Both of them used their meager talents to supplement the family income in the bleak Midland years, when repeated pregnancies competed with the struggle to earn a living.

At that the girls were better off than their parents, Patrick and Ann Crawford, and other relatives back home in Dublin, who had been left in destitution by the collapse of the textile business. Ida's maternal grandfather Patrick, the baker, did not survive it long; he died in 1827, only a year after the removal of the tariff protection. A few years later, three of his four daughters could be counted in England, all married to young Irishmen who had followed the flight of the textile trade.

The movements of the Walshes and the O'Connors through the Midlands have already been traced. It was a migratory progress from one textile town to another. Sometimes they lived together or near one another in the same city; then they would be separated again. Children were born, responsibilities increased, and living became more difficult, one supposes, until the families concluded that life could be no worse, and might conceivably be a great deal better if they took the daring gamble of going to America. They must have heard the stories of fortunes to be made in America, of gold in the streets, of plentiful jobs—wild tales circulated all over the British Isles and Europe in those days.

Fortunately for them, the Walshes and O'Connors did not sail for New York, where most of the Irish were clustering. They went to that other Mecca of their countrymen, Boston, but had the good sense to get out of the city into the country, where jobs were a little more plentiful and living, although perhaps no more rewarding financially, was at least far better than the Boston slums, and better in any case than the grimy Midland cities from which they had come.

They would have had to look a long way for a more pleasant place to settle than Salem, where the O'Connors came to rest. Its rural New England charms must have seemed a far cry from Manchester and Leeds. Whatever happy memories of her childhood Ellen had were centered in the years when the O'Connor house was the habitual meeting place for the girl children.

Not all of those years could have been happy ones, however. Ellen was probably six or seven when she came to America with her family; she was not quite nineteen when, according to what we were able to learn, she arrived in New York. In between, at twelve, she is said to have gone into domestic service. The basis for this belief is her disappearance from the 1855 Malden census records, as well as a story told in the family.

There is good reason to suppose it is true. The Walshes had not done well in America. Thomas was eventually compelled to go to San Francisco and start a new life without his family, and there is little doubt that those at home had to support themselves as best they could. Ellen's mother Ann could still work as a milliner. Her daughter Mary and her son Michael were still too young to be put into any kind of service. Only Ellen was the right age, for those days, when poor girls often had to work as domestics before they were barely adolescent.

Those seven years between Ellen's twelfth and twentieth birthdays remain the most mysterious part of her life. Nothing she left behind her sheds any positive light on that interval. There were a few family stories. She and her cousin went to the fortune teller, and she was much admired for her good looks. In the family portraits she appears as a beautiful, dark, intense girl.

There can be only speculation about those years, but the few fragments which are available suggest a plausible theory, while at the same time raising even more tantalizing questions. The family story was that she went to work in a rich man's family named Johnston, or Johnson, where the young and handsome son Harvey fell in love with her, to the chagrin of his parents, who thought a servant girl was beneath him. Nevertheless, so the story goes, Harvey persisted. He meant to educate her to the point where he could marry her without risking disgrace.

Harvey must have done well. How else can one account for Ida Wood's obvious evidences of culture, which were plain from the beginning of her married life with Ben Wood? A rich man's home in those days meant almost always that it was a place of refinement as well. Even if Harvey had not ministered to her educational needs, she could hardly have avoided absorbing at least a part of the atmosphere. But judging from the other refinements she later displayed, there must have been some tutoring.

It is also possible that Harvey Johnson was more than a friend to Ellen. As his family could no doubt have testified, it would have been unreasonable to believe that a young and beautiful servant girl could grow up in a house without attracting the attention and solicitude of its male members. If Harvey's intentions were so serious that he was contemplating marriage as soon as Ellen could be educated to a new station in life, it is not hard to believe that during the interval of transformation, Ellen ripened from an awkward twelve-year-old to a lovely nineteen.

Out of these speculations rises another theory, a bold one, but carrying with it a certain plausibility in view of subsequent events. The pivotal year in Ellen's life was 1857, when she apparently arrived in New York. That was the year Emma was born, on February 10. Is it possible that Emma was, in fact, Ellen's daughter—the illegitimate child of Harvey Johnson?

There was, to begin with, every reason to falsify Emma's birth if she were illegitimate. Family shame would dictate it, not only of Ellen's family but of the Johnsons, who were said to have opposed the whole affair. The birth certificate, of course, names the parents as Thomas and Ann Walsh, but certainly falsification of such a record would not be beyond a woman like Ellen, who made a career of deception, nor even of her mother, who willingly abetted that deception. Granted that this particular maneuver would have posed some formidable problems, they were no more difficult than the ones Ellen subsequently surmounted.

If this theory is true, it would account for Ellen's anxiety to take Emma into her own family, and pass her off as Ben Wood's child. That must have been the most complicated of her transformations, and it was the one that represented the greatest threat to her grand scheme. There were constant intimations during her marriage, emanating from Ben's enemies, that there was something strange about Emma. If anyone had succeeded in exposing this fraud, and we must presume that there were a good many people who would have been delighted to do it, the whole deception might well have been exposed.

Nevertheless, Ellen insisted on taking Emma as soon as she had a home for her. Why? If Emma were really the child of Ida's mother, why should the mother have given her up? That would not have been necessary to further the deception of Ann's transformation into a Mayfield. Emma would have been better off being Emma Mayfield, and her proper age, instead of an Emma Wood ten years older than advertised. Nor was it a question of money. Ida Wood was as well able to take care of a sister as a daughter. No reasonable explanation offers itself for this deception other than a mother's wish to have her own child, and the peculiar circumstances were the only ones open to Ellen to make it possible.

If Ben Wood believed that Emma was really Ida's sister, that too was logical. She would certainly not want him to think that she had had an illegitimate daughter, although he could hardly have cast the first stone, considering that he may well have had the same kind of affair to deal with in the person of the mysterious Delia.

There remains the question of the faded valentine which Ida Wood treasured and kept until her death, with its acrostic, "Dearest Ida Mayfield." Although the date on it is February 14, 1857, it is quite unlikely that Ellen was in possession of it then, and it is equally unlikely that Ben Wood gave it to her. She did not begin using the Mayfield name until much later. In fact, for the next ten years, she posed as "Mrs. Harvey." How did she acquire the valentine, then?

The most reasonable explanation is that it came from one of the places where she worked during the period before she met Ben, a period during which she presumably supported herself by working as a domestic.

No doubt Ellen cherished that valentine as a lovely object in itself, and eventually the name in it may have suggested itself to her as a name which she might adopt. After her creation of the fictitious Mayfields, she possibly kept it as supporting evidence, if it were ever needed, since it was dated ten years before her official marriage.

It was a precarious life that Ellen led at first in New York. The Irish, who had arrived in New York in successive waves of immigration in the first four decades of the century, had been jammed into a huge slum area. They were exploited by landlords and employers alike, crowded into indescribable tenements, kept as poor and illiterate as possible, and left to stew in their own misery. Their vast ghetto stretched from the barren railroad flats of Rivington Street and the Five Points to the shacks of Goat Hill on the undulating slopes of mid-island. They were treated with disdain by the entrenched business and social groups, themselves composed of immigrants or the children of immigrants. "No dogs or Irish allowed," read the sign in many respectable restaurants and hotels.

Ida possibly lived in this environment, and if this be so it may serve as an additional explanation for her efforts to conceal her Irish background. It cannot be determined precisely when Ida started to call herself Mrs. Harvey. Emma was taken down to New York to visit "Mrs. Harvey" during the next few years, or so the neighbors and relatives were given to understand, and presumably this was the Ellen they had known. But the Harvey name does not appear on any official document until April 12, 1864, when she bought the house at 213 West Fifty-fourth Street as Ida Harvey, which suggests that she had already begun to think of herself as Ida instead of Ellen.

Ellen had been in New York a short time when she wrote her brazen letter to Ben Wood, about whom she had heard, evidently, from a girl who had been a previous mistress. She signed it "Nellie," using a nickname which it appears her mother called her on occasion.

The letter may seem a cold-blooded approach, but if we assume certain facts to be true, it is at least understandable in the light of Ellen's previous life. She had known poverty and struggle from her earliest days; they were traditions in her family.

There must have been a fierce determination within her that this new life would not be a repetition of the cruel battle for existence that she and her family had known. She wanted money, not for what it would buy, as her subsequent actions proved, but for the security it represented. She had the normal human female desire to wear fine clothes and lead the good life, but in the end it was money as security that shaped all her actions.

She was certainly aware that her beauty could be the means of getting what she wanted. A good many people had remarked about her good looks, and she was conscious of them. At ninety-four, only a few months before her death, she was still trying to preserve the delicate complexion which had been one of the marks of her striking appearance.

Armed with her beauty, she was ready when the target moved into view. Hearing about Ben Wood from the other girl gave her the courage and determination to write and find out if she could not be his "new face." She must have been certain in her mind that if she could only arrange a meeting with Ben, the rest would be easy. She could not have foreseen, or even anticipated, what happened. Ben Wood, in search of a new mistress, found love.

There can be no question that his love for Ida was the one shining, almost obsessive element in Ben's life. He demonstrated it in countless ways, and his letters give expression to it. Whether Ida returned his devotion is more difficult to say. It would be pleasant to believe that this, too, was the one great, overwhelming, honest emotion of her life. Perhaps it was. But it is easier to take the view that her devotion to Ben was based far more on the realization of her ambitions.

At least twice in their married life, Ben was in financial trouble rising from his large-scale gambling, and had to appeal to his thrifty wife for help. She gave him the money he needed, but the documents we found in Ida's effects and other evidence showed she always got something in return—stocks or other assets in Ben's portfolio. On the last occasion, she got his newspaper. These, if the facts stated in writing on the subject are taken at face value, are not the unselfish acts of a woman devoted to her husband.

My own belief has been that the sale of the controlling stock interest in the newspaper was no more than a token transfer designed to place the *Daily News* outside the reach of Ben's creditors. Ben was left penniless, and shortly afterward he died, and his will was never probated, because it was planned that way. The acts of ownership over the newspaper Ida performed were done to give apparent substance to the transfer, all under the private direction of Ben, who never visited the newspaper premises after the transfer but continued as editor-in-chief to write the paper's editorials from his rooms at the Fifth Avenue Hotel.

Whatever the basis of the relationship between Ida and Ben, and in what emotional balance it may have been, they were inseparable from the beginning. It could not have been easy at the start. There was Ben's ambiguous domestic situation in Manhasset, where he may or may not have been married to the woman he later called Delia Bowers, but who was then listed in the census as Delia Wood, and presumably bore him a child of the same name who came to live with Ben and Ida after the older Delia's death.

After he met Ida, Ben no longer had any time for the family in Manhasset, whatever the circumstances. He must have seen her constantly, and unquestionably lived with her, in the usual meaning of the term, whether it was or was not an arrangement sanctioned by the Philadelphia minister, as Ida claimed. Was it Delia Wood's death which set Ben free in 1867? Then they could be married in the church of Ida's faith. Then Ben could bring the young girl who was his daughter by Delia Wood to live with him, and Ida could bring into this strange household her own daughter, Emma, if that was the case. But where Ben could be vague about little Delia, Ida could not, under the circumstances, be as vague about Emma.

Judging by the letter Ben wrote to Father Young when he was disturbed about his will, he himself may have been one of the deceived, if he really believed that Emma was Ida's sister. The reference in another letter to having Ida in his care since she was fifteen may have been still another deception, a puzzling one.

But as soon as the marriage took place in 1867, the great impersonation began in earnest. In Benjamin Wood's company for the past ten years Ida had been "Mrs. Harvey," or "Ida Harvey." Now she signed the marriage register boldly as a Mayfield. Sometime during that decade, she had decided to give herself a family background that would not create any social difficulties for Ben Wood. It would have been one thing for Ben to marry an obscure Mrs. Harvey, whose family background was doubtful. It was quite another for him to take as wife the charming daughter of a rich Louisiana sugar planter, a man of substance, whose lineage could be traced to the nobility. Thus Ellen Walsh burst upon the social world in which her husband moved as a transplanted Southern belle of unquestioned background.

The hard question which remains impenetrable to any documented analysis is how she managed the transition from Mrs. Harvey to Ida Mayfield, if she had been well known in Ben's company by the first name. One can only speculate that the use of "Mrs. Harvey" on documents was misleading, and that in reality during the decade before her marriage she was already calling herself Ida Mayfield.

In a later period of time Ida might not have been able to succeed in her masquerade. Society was still in a disorganized state in New York in 1867. New fortunes were being made rapidly; it was hard to tell new money from old money, and sharp distinctions had not yet been made between "blood" and "money" in establishing social rank.

But society accepted Ida Mayfield Wood, as it accepted a good many other women of uncertain background. If its members had any reason to doubt her story, they did not make a point of it. One wonders how Ida overcame the most obvious difficulty in transforming Walshes to Mayfields—the absence of an authentic Louisiana, Southern accent in the voices of these Mayfields, who must have spoken in the distinctive Irish-New England voice which so easily identifies South Boston today.

There must have been some who wondered about that, but if so, there was never any trouble. Ida was an accepted member of society—or of that part of it which accepted her husband. There may have been relatively few social leaders who did so at the beginning, but as the passions of the war died down, and as the *Daily News* began to make Ben a rich man, her place in the general social scheme was secure. One may be sure that Emma's coming-out party at Delmonico's was attended by the people who mattered.

The deception flowered quickly after her marriage. Emma was almost immediately a part of the household. Her sister Mary had never been very far from her at any point; their lives were so closely interwoven at every point that her transformation to being a Mayfield was the easiest part of the entire scheme. As soon as Ellen became Ida Mayfield Wood, Mary at once was Mary E. Mayfield without question. It was necessary, too, for Ida to take over the fortunes of her young brother Michael, who was sent off to school and later became Henry Mayfield. He was never a complicating factor. The final touch was to bring her mother to New York, after her brother Louis's unfortunate drowning, and make her the widow of Thomas Henry Mayfield, of Louisiana.

While ambition and insecurity were the prime factors in Ellen's magnificent hoax, it must be said in her favor that she treated her family with the utmost consideration, particularly her mother, on whom she lavished affection and comfort during the thirteen years she spent with her mother before her death. That Ellen was profoundly affected by her mother's loss is shown in her grandiose plans for the monument in Calvary Cemetery, on which there eventually appeared the full extent of her fiction: Her brother Michael Walsh as Henry Benjamin Mayfield; Thomas Walsh, her father, as Thomas Henry Mayfield; and her mother, Ann Crawford Walsh, as Ann Crawford Mayfield, widow of Thomas Henry; along with those children gone before.

In the end, the perpetrator of the hoax and her two chief victims survived. For in securing her own place in life, Ellen Walsh had conceived a fraud which was not without its losses as well as its gains. She brought happiness to Ben Wood, and she gratified her own ambitions, but the insecurity was too deeply implanted to be eradicated, and eventually it drove her into being a recluse and a miser in her old age.

It ought to be said, in defense of Ellen, that she did not become a recluse—she did not "withdraw," to use the professional term employed by psychiatrists and others who have made studies of recluses—all at once. Nor was her hoarding of money entirely unnatural, at least at the outset.

In my many years of experience as counsel to the Public Administrator and more recently as Surrogate, I have encountered literally hundreds of cases of "withdrawal." Often I have been tempted to generalize in my own mind about recluses, but whatever the particular generalization might have been in my mind at the time, it was jarred by new experiences with each new case involving a recluse. For each human being is unique, his habits and reactions molded by the interaction of forces that have not yet been fully probed

—habits and reactions conditioned by inherited or acquired characteristics, ambitions, hardships, and frustrations.

When Ellen moved to the Herald Square Hotel, there is no evidence that she had determined to seclude herself entirely from society, with Emma and Mary as her sole companions. She felt financially secure enough to travel, and the activities of her contemporaries no doubt held sufficient interest for her, even though she now regarded herself as a person apart. In her last years, however, she was indeed a recluse. Along with Emma and Mary, she had isolated herself from the outside world, she had divorced herself from fellow human beings except for obtaining essential needs. Emma, dominated all her life by Ellen, unquestioningly joined her in retirement; Mary yielded because she knew no life other than the one she shared with Ida.

There are certain things we know about Ida which help to explain her becoming a recluse. It seems clear, for example, that she had formed no close friendships during the long years of her seemingly gay, at all events active, participation in the social and political affairs of New York City while Ben was alive, apparently because she lived in constant apprehension that her deceptions might be found out, and her true origin and identity discovered. It was Mary, not Ellen, who visited Aunt Eliza in Salem, Massachusetts. Obviously instructed to do so, Mary concealed Ida's new name or her whereabouts from Aunt Eliza, never visited her again, and Ellen failed to send the gift to Aunt Eliza which Mary had promised. Fear that her hoax might be discovered also played a large part in Ellen's refusal to allow access to her apartment at the Herald Square, particularly to its inner room.

Her hoarding of money was not the act of a feeble mind, though her judgment was apparently overpowered by fear. The advice she received about the Panic of 1907 led her to distrust banks. Until 1928 she and her sisters maintained a box in a bank vault, where she apparently kept her cash. That her judgment on this score was not completely warped may also be found in the fact that she held on to the sound security, the Union Pacific bonds. Physical debilitation and fear of not being able to reach the bank vault undoubtedly led to taking the money and securities out of the box and hiding them in the rooms at the Herald Square. Then, too, her self-confidence was sapped by her inability to make a go of it as the owner of the *Daily News*.

Shrewdness and self-protection induced by fear, not eccentricity or a weakened mentality, caused her to plead poverty to the doctor who came to minister to Mary, to the undertaker who came to attend to Mary's burial, and to the Herald Square bellboy who bought Ida's daily food. None of them knew or even suspected she was a woman of wealth, because she successfully carried on her masquerade of impoverishment.

As the generation of which she considered herself a part receded in time, her interests in her surroundings lessened. She regarded herself as a Walsh, not identifying herself with the Wood family, certainly not with any fictitious Mayfields, else she would not have preserved the writings and other memoranda which helped ultimately to establish her true identity. As Surrogate Foley said in the decision given after he had heard the evidence on the Walsh-Mayfield conflict: "It is the jest of fortune that having attained wealth and prominence, she abandoned her pretense at the age of sixty, and retired to strict seclusion. By way of direct contrast, during her last years in the talks and writings (which she preserved) she cherishes only the memory of her real parents and her Walsh and Crawford lineage."

But Ellen's memories of her family were not calculated to bring her happiness. In the years of seclusion at the Herald Square, she could remember only that she had abandoned her relatives, and now it was too late to make amends. If, as appears, she had a close emotional attachment to them which she sacrificed in satisfying her ambitions, she may have suffered guilt feelings which intensified her drawing away from a world filled with strangers. That she doomed Emma and Mary to following her own course, forsaking contact with close relations, was not calculated to bring her anything but additional unhappiness in her lonely reflections upon her past.

Public understanding of recluses comes largely from newspaper accounts of those wealthy ones who lived out the last years of their life as misers. Such people are pictured as eccentrics, and in view of the wealth which they leave behind, are looked upon with curiosity rather than sympathy, for "withdrawal" is by no means the exclusive domain of the wealthy or of eccentrics. Most recluses die paupers. They become mere names, dates, and places in unpublished medical examiners' or coroners' reports, and many of them are buried in municipal cemeteries.

People who live alone, and die alone, rarely do so voluntarily. There are as many different stories as there are recluses, and it is impossible to say that aloneness is evidence of being one—that is, a voluntary retirement from associating with other human beings. Suspicion or an unnatural sense of independence are often cited as other causes, but as in the case of Ida, they begin to predominate after other things have occurred, such as the loss of loved ones, or other hurts that cannot be overcome.

Then, in a kind of paralysis of mind or emotion that we have never been able really to understand, the recluse loses all sense of responsibility. Ellen no longer cared whether the will she had executed in 1889 remained valid or not. She had no interest in making a new one. She was passionately devoted to maintaining her hoard, but she had apparently long ago forgotten why. If acquiring money meant she had to bestir herself even slightly, she remained inactive, as when she failed over a period of years to cash the interest coupons on her Union Pacific bonds. Her mind was directed inward, toward herself. The world outside was full of hostile people, but she was no longer intrigued by the challenge of conquering them as she was when, a lovely girl of nineteen, she came to New York City to achieve her ambitions.

It was her own daughter, Emma, if she was, and her own sister Mary who were the victims of Ellen's dominating personality, and her withdrawal from active life. Perhaps there could have been no other way for Emma. Her unfortunate deformity gave her an initial handicap which might have been hard to overcome, and it could be said she was fortunate to be sheltered by a rich sister. But sheltered she was, and dominated, and never a real person through her unhappy life until she died. The cruel necessity of being ten years younger than she was created further problems which she could not have understood. Poor Emma. In those two words were a summation of her life and an epitaph.

As for Mary, the evidence would seem to indicate that she was the best balanced of them all. If she did not have her sister's compelling beauty, she was nevertheless a good-looking young woman. Yet she was as submerged by Ellen's dominant personality as the others, and completely submitted her life to her sister. Why? No one knows. She went quietly about her own affairs, performing whatever Ellen asked of her. How much did she know about her sister's tangled affairs? Presumably everything, but she was utterly loyal. Ellen never had the slightest reason to fear her.

Mary remains, in a way, more of a puzzle than Ellen, for she could certainly have found a husband, and lived her own life. Even in her old age, she was said to attract attention when she walked in New York with her graceful, free-swinging stride, wearing her out-of-date clothes which somehow still looked stylish. A handsome woman of intelligence and charm who chose to submerge her own life in her sister's and live in almost complete anonymity—that was Mary Walsh, an enigma to the end.

If Ellen is not so much a puzzle when the pieces of her life are put together, she remains by far the most fascinating figure in the case. To conceive and carry out a deception on so splendid a scale marks her as a woman of steadfast purpose, iron determination, and native intelligence.

As the search for Ida Wood remains unique in the annals of litigation over estates, so does Ellen Walsh stand almost alone among her contemporaries who struggled to establish themselves in the world of the nineteenth century. Few women faced greater odds; even fewer succeeded as well.